# Sons Must Die and Other Plays

AF631384

## South Asian Canadian Literature Series

*General Editor*: Uma Parameswaran

| | |
|---|---|
| **SACLIT 1** | **Trishanku and Other Writings**<br>Uma Parameswaran |
| **SACLIT 2** | **Sons Must Die and Other Plays**<br>Uma Parameswaran |
| **SACLIT 3** | **Five or Six Characters in Search of Toronto and Other Plays**<br>Rana Bose |
| **SACLIT 4** | **Land Where the Trees Talk and Other Plays**<br>Rahul Varma |

# Sons Must Die and Other Plays

UMA PARAMESWARAN

PRESTIGE

*Published by*
Prestige Books
3/28, East Patel Nagar
New Delhi 110 008

1998

ISBN: 81-7551-020-X

© Uma Parameswaran

*Cover design*: Leelavati Bagavant

*Art format*: Vinod Bakshi

*Photo Typesetting by*
Pivot Computers
Delhi 110 006
Ph. 2934490

*Printed at*
Chaman Offset Printers
New Delhi 110 002

# Contents

## Author's Statement
# First Person Singular

When I was a child, my imagination soared into strange skies, but they seem always to have had a streak of humour and social commentary. For example, the story that won a prize in one of the annual *Shankar's Weekly* competitions was titled "How Mahesh Went to Heaven," and it started with God being so surprised that anyone should call him in this day and age that he appears in person and grants Mahesh his wish to visit heaven. Later, I remember, I wrote a parody of the custom of "bride-inspection" where a young woman interviewed prospective bridegrooms.

Humour is absent in much of my published writings, partly because I have not sent too many pieces in search of a market, and partly because Canadian editors just don't seem interested in humour when it comes from a non-white immigrant, who is needless to say expected to write of pain and discrimination etc. But one of these days, voila, my Maru stories will see the light of day as a volume, though I doubt I can write any more dramatic scripts that are humorous. Satire perhaps, may be.

The plays included in this volume have been written over three decades, and represent different phases of my writing career. All of them are serious, and often intense.

*Sons Must Die* was written long ago—in 1962. I had always loved long narrative poems—Macaulay's *Lays of Ancient Rome*, Longfellow's *Hiawatha*, Matthew Arnold's *Sohrab and Rustum,* Tennyson. . . . In the early 1960s, I was steeped in Milton and had recently discovered the Greek tragedians. I lived in Nagpur at the time. The India-China War of 1962 had an impact on me, as it did on almost every young person at the time. There is something heady about going to war, something that makes one romanticize, perhaps unduly, thanks to poems with which I grew up: Tennyson's "Breathes there a man with soul so dead . . ." and Macaulay's "And how can man die better than facing fearful odds, for the ashes of his fathers and the temples of his gods?" There was an outburst of patriotism. Old pre-Independence marching songs were revived: "Khilenge phool iss jagah mein watan ke naam shahid ho." Women's organizations mobilized help in all kinds of ways. Newspapers passed from hand to hand, and were read over shoulders. People clustered in pin drop silence around radios at tea-shops and street corners. Everyone I knew went at least once to the railway station to cheer our khaki-clad jawans who packed the trains on the Grand Trunk tracks that carried them from the south to the battlefront. Several families I knew lost sons; the impact came close to home when young women at our college lost brothers, and one her husband.

But to delineate the horrors of war, I had to distance myself from the engulfing patriotic fervour of 1962.

*Sons Must Die* is set against the backdrop of Kashmir and the India-Pakistan war of 1947-1948. The concept of the sub-continent as a cultural entity has been in our blood for centuries, but the concept of "political entity" was still beyond some of the older generation at a time when shifting borders rather than long-nurtured village relationships dictated who was enemy and who an ally. This I tried to reflect through the three women in the play, each coming from a different part of the sub-continent, all unfamiliar with the geographical and political realities of Kashmir. Their maternal sensibility transcends political boundaries and sees only what Wilfred Owen calls the "pity of war."

Then I left India on a Smith-Mundt Fulbright scholarship, to study American Literature at Indiana University.

Two years later, when I came to Canada with my husband, I got caught up in the settlement phase that most immigrants go through. I see four phases in the personal histories of South Asian Canadians up to the 1980s, phases that also have a corresponding pattern in the collective context. The phases are: first, wonder and fear at the new world around oneself, and nostalgia for the world left behind; second, an overriding impulse to survive in the new environment which makes one immerse oneself in one's career or family, and often precludes political or social participation in the larger society; third, after one has found job security, a turning towards organizational activity within one's own ethnocentric community; and finally, an active participation in the larger political and social arena. Individuals might stay different lengths of time in each phase; also, at the collective level, though the community collectively goes through the same pattern, there is some diversity. At any given time there are large numbers of individuals in each of the phases since immigration of new members is a continuing phenomenon.

In the personal context of immigrants' experience, the first phase is both a pleasure and a nightmare, as they strive paradoxically to grab with open hands the best of both worlds. Though the landscape around us was spruce and pine, the landscape of memory was filled with jasmine and mango. Thus, in the first collective phase, collective cultural activity revolved around the latter—nostalgia that took the form of attempts to transplant our old familiar environment on to Canadian soil. At various community events organized around India's Independence Day, Republic Day, Holi and Deepavali, adult men and women of Indian descent sang and danced, and enacted plays. While the songs and scripts were usually imported from India, there were a few of us who tried to create our own.

My own early scripts, of which *Meera* is an example, were written in this context. *Meera* is a script that evolved around our artistic resources, and set out to celebrate Indian art traditions and at the same time to educate the outsider about our culture. Written in 1971, it has a very simple story line that takes us through Meera's life with all its familiar episodes. It gives us the pleasure of the familiar, while telling outsiders basic details about Krishna's life and our dance and music traditions. It was produced in 1972 by Rubena Sinha (who had studied dance with Uday Shankar and was one of our main "resources") for the fledgling Hindu Society of Manitoba, which sponsored the stage production.

But it must be remembered that each artistic creation is also an expression of the writer's vision, and my references to T.S. Eliot and Christopher Marlowe reveal what I call dual cultural sensibility. The theme is lofty; it affirms the power of faith and the spiritual space afforded by art; but the actual stage presentation made clear that the script took into account the limited resources that we as a small community had at the time.

A digression, if I may, since I have spent much energy over the years on matters concerning the Indian diaspora in Canada. The Indo-Canadian community (a vast majority of brown people in Manitoba at the time were from India, and hardly a handful from other South Asian countries,) was young, numerically small, and talented. Most of us were in white collar professions. Many of the women had some proficiency and practical experience in one or more of: vocal music, instrumental music, classical or folk dance, painting and ceramics, besides the usual and unusual culinary skills. It was an aesthetic joy to see the flexibility of the body evident in the *raasa, garbha,* and *bhangra* dances that we staged, a flexibility that one loses in the westernized daily routine where the body does not have to bend when doing the daily chores around the house. Today, in the 1990s, our performers, who are younger than we were at that time, seem to have lost that flexibility. Also, we do not seem to have any adult immigrant women on our community stages in Winnipeg. Our events feature only children and youth born in Canada. Where are the adult performers? It could not be, surely, that they, collectively, do not have the same talents that we collectively had at their age. The law of probability suggests that there should be about as many talented newcomers as we had in our early days. Have the new adult immigrants been marginalized by the younger generation of performers born here?

If so, I am partly responsible, albeit unintentionally, both as a 1960s immigrant and as an individual. In the mid 1970s, most of us had young children who were born here. We did what conscientious parents everywhere do. We drove them to classes—swimming, skating, ballet, gymnastics, ice hockey, junior league, piano, band. When my daughter was seven, I decided to work towards bringing Bharata Natyam dance lessons to Winnipeg. There had been brief one-time workshops with visiting dancers but I wanted more. I wanted the same continuity and professionalism that our children had in their other extra-curricular activities. In April, 1978, I managed to organize a month-long dance instruction course taught by a senior dance teacher trained in Madras, Mrs. Sarasi Raj of Montreal. It was the first organized dance-instruction programme in Canada that brought a teacher from out of town, and it continued twice a year for three years. I wrote *Sita's Promise* for the *arangetram* so to say, of the first graduates. It was staged at the Winnipeg Art Gallery on April 25, 1981.

*Sita's Promise* belongs to the first collective phase of Indo-Canadian experience, though in the personal chart, it falls in the third phase, namely, the phase in which a well-settled immigrant turns to contributing to the intersections of one's community-affiliations and one's larger Canadian identity.

The play links epic India with modern Canada through myth and dance. Rama, Sita and Lakshmana—the main characters in the *Ramayana*—during their forest exile find a wounded Arctic tern that has lost its way in its northern migration. They resolve to take it back to its home; they travel northwards through India to the Himalayas, where Jatayu, the sacred eagle, carries them to the tern's home by the shores of the primeval ocean that we now call Lake Agassiz. The native children dance for Sita and ask her to stay with them. Sita says she must go but promises them that she will come again, "I through my people shall surely come again, and we shall . . . sing our songs with the children of all the different lands who make this their home."

The story is purely imaginary. Its only point of coincidence with the original epic is that Rama was exiled for fourteen years. The characterization of Rama is interpretive, not traditional. It traces Rama's growth from a narrow preoccupation with codes of kingship to an awareness of what it is to be human to a point where he rises to realize his divine mission. The drama ends with our recognition of Rama as the avatar of Vishnu, the Supreme Essence.

*Dear Deedi, My Sister* was composed in the 1980s, though it was in draft form much earlier. The 1980s was a decade in which I spent much time working on women's issues. I was on the Board of Immigrant Women's Association of Manitoba, and the Margaret Laurence Chair of Women's Studies, and various other committees. *Dear Deedi* uses many of the poems that are in my *Trishanku*, but names were changed to expand the "community" from Indo-Canadian to our larger immigrant community.

*Rootless but Green are the Boulevard Trees* is the only one of my Canadian plays that was written without a specific community stage in mind. I showed the script to several friends, and word got around that I was writing a play featuring real people in the Indo-Canadian community. The identity of the "real people" varied with speakers. This was understandable, because though I was not using any "real" people, I was using situations that could and did happen in average Indo-Canadian families!

What I find intriguing is that I have been living with these characters a long time, and that they keep trying to find their medium, now knocking on the doors of poetry, now of the stage, and now of fiction. *Darkest before Dawn* is the novel that they have been shaping and reshaping, and one of these days they will manage to swim on to the printed page, speaking prose.

March 1996 **UMA PARAMESWARAN**

# SONS MUST DIE

*The Vale of Kashmir. 1948 A.D.*

*The Curtain rises on the Chorus of Old Men. They wear traditional Kashmiri dress. The cut of their beards and their caps show that two of them are Hindus, one a Sikh, the other eight, Muslims. In the background is a slope dotted with pine trees and cottages. The snowline is visible in the distance.*

Chorus: Kashmir! Valley beloved of the Great!
Many have been the wars fought here
These two thousand years.
Fratricidal wars for all wars are fratricidal,
No hollow platitude—all men ARE brothers.
Many were the hands that held your sceptre
Varied the faiths of your rulers.

From the north came Kushans, the Scythian sword
Sweeping o'er these vales. . . .
Noble Harsha, last of a glorious race, ruled you
And then came dynasties—Karkota, Utpala, Gupta—
And the long line of Hindu kings ended
When the land was seized
By that Muslim warrior, Shah Mirza,
Whose scion found favour with Tamerlane.
Sons of Islam kept you a long time—adventurers
Whose zeal for faith spurred them to scale perilous cliffs,
Face roaring seas, leaving their desert land,
Their homes and caravans to spread Islam.
Great were the feats that faith inspired in men
Who at sword-point spread the Prophet's creed
Till today but one of every five are outside
The fold. We have lived side by side these centuries

And our poets and monarchs forged our common bonds;
Zain ul Abidin the enlightened king who recalled
The ousted Brahmins to translate the epics
So men may know other faiths, and knowing,
Still retain their own. Truly worthy was he
Of the name we give him now—Akbar-e-Kashmir.
Akbar whose imperial sway too you have seen
And all his line till with the Abdali you felt
The Afghan power that gave place to the warriors
Of the Nanak fraternity who traded
Much of you away to the whiteman
Who from across the seas founded an empire
Which never saw the set of sun.

And they leaving, our new western neighbour marched in
And our king called Bharat to his aid and merged you
Into the new and powerful state
(for it is well that small ones unite
to form a great and glorious whole.)

Since then there has been war
A long and wearying fight o'er thee
(ay who will not fight for so fair a land?)
O Kashmir, what is yet to be?
Beloved vale, could we but know what is to be!

Too beautiful are you to suffer thus. And yet
Suffering has been your lot. Poor you have been
Always, dear mother, your people
Ever exploited by traders from the plains,
Your mountain tribes wandering with their herd
To find grassy meads to feed their flocks
And so them.

Poor did I say? ah me mother, your pardon I crave.
Poor you may be in what men call wealth, but rich
Rich are you in treasures loved by the Great.
Nature's favourite realm where she unstintingly

Showers all her splendour on land and man,
Man to whom is given skillful hands
To weave shawls and fabrics beyond compare.
(ay I labour at them night and day
and the trader takes them away for princesses
leaving me no more than a day's broth.)
And my eyes have grown dim at these handicrafts
So dim I could not see this figure from afar.
Close it has come, a woman it is;
What strange apparel is this?
A sari such as women wear, yet not so worn.
Many come here I have not seen before.
An Indian she seems. I'll soon know more.

*Enter from right, Meenakshi. Her dark red sari of Conjeevaram silk is wrapped in Tamil Brahmin style. She comes with slow steps, looking all around, at the snow-capped peaks, the valley, the sky. She does not heed the Chorus who step back.*

Meenakshi: Kashmir? This the valley beloved of the gods?
Likely so for 'tis beautiful, aye a pity 'tis so beautiful,
For its beauty causes war. A beautiful woman
Beautiful, too too much so.
The playground of the gods she is called.
Ye gods, why do you not keep her for yourselves?
Or is it that our battle here is play for you,
That you allow such discord in this vale?

My son, my son! where are you?
This enchantress has lured you away. It was ever
Your wish to fly high into the clouds, and here
The clouds girdle the vale below.
Are you satisfied, my son?
As you lie in the arms of this siren
Does she keep you warm, my son?
She looks so cold to me. . . .
And yet it was your desire to fly here.
And even as I caught you in that last embrace

I did not hold you but an empty frame
Decked in blue serge and a star.
Your heart was already here, your mind's eye
Seeing below the plane you piloted
This place, this wretched, beautiful place.
My son. . . o my little one! (*she sobs*)

Chorus: Do you remember the whirr we heard nightly,
The small specks we saw flying steadily overhead?
Those were planes from Delhi, planes and paratroopers
Who land we know not where, and join their comrades
To keep watch on our frontier.
And such a pilot is her son mayhaps. Poor woman
Who cannot see beauty for her tears. But forgive her
For it is her mother heart that cries.

Meenakshi: Two thousand miles I have travelled
For you. Come to me, my darling child.
O why did you come here?

Chorus: His country ordered him to.

Meenakshi: Why? Why?

Chorus: To keep this fair land.

Meenakshi: Fair land? is my land not fair?
Does it not stretch two thousand miles
From the Western Sea to the Bay? Does it not
Embrace the forests and plains from Himalaya
To Kanya Kumari? And are those not fair?
Verdurous fields have we whose green splendour
Mellows tired eyes resting in the afternoon sun.
And what sunshine! Trees. Have we not trees?
What charm is there in these needle pines
That stand bleak against the white?
Ours are trees that shower fruits:
Mangoes, oranges, neem; peepal trees

That catch every sigh of the passing breeze,
Under whose shade our gods are worshipped;
Tall coconut palms that rise slender into the sky
Bearing nectar; eucalyptus that whisper sweet lullaby
And cool the sun rays into soft breeze.
O what is here we do not have?

Chorus: Snow-capped peaks
Where one glimpses Eternity.

Meenakshi: Ah, in my Madras I stand on the washed sands
And hear Infinity lapping at my feet.
Warm are the waves that break on our beach
Where, in days gone by, I have sat by my son
As he built moats in the sand. My darling,
My child! Where are you?

Chorus: Here we see static Eternity in its strength,
There she sees the Infinite.
Are they not one? Both of the Supreme?

Meenakshi: What do you say? I cannot hear you.
Your voice comes as from a well, for my ears
Are attuned only to catch the sound of the plane
That he pilots through the air.
I know nothing but that I love my son,
And he a wanderer, wrecked perhaps,
Fighting for a region we need not have
Though ours by right it may be.
My country as it stands commands the sea,
Land, air, o why do they want more?
My India is wide enough, plenteous enough,
Rich enough, aye confused enough too
To want more. Enough have we of riches
Enough of troubles. We need no more,
And more will surely accrue even from victory.
And from loss—I dread to think—

O what amounts we stake for this!
Lives, human lives, sons' lives, O India
Is this enchantress worth sons' lives?
My son, my son, o my little one!

**Chorus:** From the way she weeps, her salt tears
Staining her brown cheeks, her hair dishevelled,
Her hands trembling so she scarce can lift
Her sari cloth to her face, one would think
The demon of hatred dwelt within;
And yet she speaks more weighty words than she knows.
Ah me, could we but know what is to be.

*Meenakshi goes to the rear while they are speaking. She slumps down, weeping. Zohra Begum enters from the right and advances to the front. She wears a* salwar-kameez *suit with gold embroidery on the blue velvet. A tinselled* chunni *covers her head. The Chorus greet her in Muslim fashion, bowing with their right hand raised to the forehead. She returns the greeting and stands silent for a moment staring at the slope.*

**Zohra Begum:** At last I have reached Kashmir. Where
My gallant sons have fallen and their father.
They were sturdy. My heart
Fair burst with pride looking at them—
He with a son on either side
Discussing deals planned or made—
As they returned for evening prayer.
Tall and handsome, straight nose,
Bold eyes below broad forehead,
Beards clipped neat.
Happy days!

A mound of snow
No marble tomb.
No dirge.
No incense chant.

He loved an even tenor.
Wanted things in place.
Took inventory Monday mornings.
Yes, so ordered, so set in his ways.
Yet he upset the entire routine of life
And went to war willingly.
Strange how patriotism moulds heroes of men!
And my sons risked that life so loved
For this valley.
Calamity, calamity
And I left with my brood of young ones.

Tokens of your bravery I have,
Sent by our kind President
Through the soldier who brought me the news of woe.
Happy is our land ruled by the learned and strong
And happy we so long as we stay within.
But new lands, why new lands? why Kashmir?
People here are of our faith I know,
But what has faith to do with politics?
What matters who rules them so long
As they bow to Islam?
Aye it is because we do not bow as our Prophet
Has decreed that our sons die.

O Ineffable Name, pardon me
And those with me
Who have failed in duty towards thee.
Send us not such mournful punishment.
Allah, Ho Allah!

*Retiring to a corner she kneels facing Mecca and starts praying. The Poet who has entered meanwhile now comes forward. He is a young Muslim, dressed in* chudidar pyjamas *and black* sherwani.

Poet: Last night the moon was red.
As I sat on the banks of the blue lake
The birds flew in from the east and said

'The moon is red tonight.'
And the swan sailed by west and I traced
The parting water as it swam and saw
The western fringe all red.
I looked up, and the sun was red,
A bloody red it was as it touched the horizon,
And where it touched, a red stream melted
And flowed down in blood. The sun set
Leaving crimson gashes in the sky. The moon rose
But I dared not look up knowing it was red.

This morning when I went to the river
I saw them floating down with the current
Men-who-were rushing down the river
With frozen blood, eyes eaten away,
Limbs maimed

Chorus: Stop, stop this morbid tale.

Poet: and one was washed ashore.
Like child Moses in the rushes he lay,
I saw his young limbs stiffened
His insides shot away

Chorus: Stop! do you call this poetry?
And yourself a poet?

Poet: A long haired poet composing ghazals
And shairees, bowing to applauding listeners.
Ha, spit on me if you will but I
Spit on them.

I too sang of such things once,
The green splendour of the valley
The majestic might of the mountains
The thunderous torrent sweeping down,
Aye of starry nights and serenades
When love surged up, and hands and lips

Secretly wooed. . .
But not now, no more, never more
For I have seen the stream of blood from the bloody sun
Flooding our vale, our Kashmir.
And mothers such as these wailing for their sons,
Sons who must die.

*Enter, from left, a European nun in the habit of the Order of St. Joseph. The fingers of her right hand roll the beads of the rosary that hangs from her black silk girdle.*

Nun: Hail Mary, full of grace, the Lord is with thee.
Blessed art thou among women and blessed
Is the fruit of thy womb, Jesus.

*She seems astonished by the sight of Zohra Begum at prayer. She looks at her curiously. She looks up and starts on seeing the Muslims in the Chorus.*

Nun: Lord! Lord Jesus, have mercy on me. (*Crosses herself.*)

Chorus: You are startled.

Nun: Ave Maria! pray for me!
You wear fez caps! And should I not be afraid?
Last month. . . . Ave Maria . . . those Pakistani soldiers . . .
our sister-convent. . .

Chorus: Come, come, not all fez wearers are Pakistanis
Nor all Pakistanis ravagers.

Nun: The imprint of fear on the human heart is deep.

Chorus: Have no fear of us. You are safe here.

Nun: Thank you then. Which way to the Convent?
That Muslim woman? She too prays?
Blessed Virgin, she prays!

Chorus: Bounteous is the faith of these women
Who leave their Alpine homes for their God,
But they have a child's mind
Cooped within their stone walls.

Nun: Hail Mary, full of grace, the Lord is with thee,
Blessed art thou among women and blessed
Is the fruit of thy womb, Jesus.

*Enter from left, Dacoit, dagger at his side, knife in hand.*

Dacoit: Ha! where is she whose purse is heavy with gold?

Chorus: Barbarian! would you waylay a woman?

Dacoit: Sure I would, if she has gold.

Chorus: Attack a servant of God?

Dacoit: God? Who is that? And where is he?
Ha, the story goes that Hiranyakashipu asked,
Kicking the pillar asked that question
    And what then, grandma?
And out of the pillar came God lion-headed
    And did he roar, grandma, grrh, did he roar?
And sucked his blood, and so, dear children,
    Tell us about the blood, grandma, the blood
Close your eyes, children, else I'll go away,
    Yes, grandma, sucked his blood
Sucked his blood
    Every drop straight from the veins
So that not a drop fell on the ground
    Because if a drop touched earth
UP
    Would RISE
Close your eyes, children,
    Ten thousand warriors armed, grandma...
So the story goes. I'll kick that round bottom

So soft and round and fleshy under that billowy skirt
So fat and yielding, cushiony soft inviting,
And then God will appear to protect the chastity
So neatly knotted in black silk cloister knot
Of his bride. Ha Ha Ha
Where is she? I could hear her inane mumbling
At her beads. Parrots that repeat—keep away, worms,
I see her, keep away, my knife is sharp and seasoned.

*He darts across to the nun who is hiding behind the Chorus. The Chorus stop him. He shrugs.*

Chorus: Leave her. She is dedicated to her god.

Dacoit: God again. There is no god. And her god. Ha,
Virgin Mary, Immaculate Conception. I too am a god
For I doubt my mother ever married.

Nun: O blasphemy! Holy Mary, Mother of God, pray for us sinners
Now and at the hour of our death. Amen.

Dacoit: Ha, look at that one
Calling on the ineffable name. Like toy birds
That peck mechanically, she bows and rises,
Bows and rises. O fartable name!

Chorus: Blasphemer! Go.

Dacoit: No pundit here? I thought it was a World Conference
Of religions. No pundit to preach about the Vedas?
To worship there in Amarnath and Badrinath
The *lingam*
Of all things to choose that
Symbol. . . (*spits*.)

*Sadhu enters from left. Clad in a leopard skin, with a brass jug in one hand and a* trishul *in the other, he looks so like the popular representation of Siva that everyone instinctively draws back.*

Dacoit: (*in a louder voice to cloak his momentary start*)
Ha, the same fake whom I passed a while ago.
You come in good time. I was telling them
There is no god. Close your ears to profanity
Like that polly there.

Sadhu: I too have often wondered if there is a God,
A self-existing Being.
Deep into the Himalayan ranges I have been
Hoping to come face to face with Him.
Naked and fasting I have sat in ice-bound caves
Far beyond Amarnath, waiting for Him.
Much else came—self-control, detachment, yoga
But He did not come.
I went back to the plains.
I saw the suffering of the world.
I said, Where he all-knowing,
All-powerful,
He will not look on this silent.
And an atheist, so withdrawn from the world of men
I could not re-enter that life, I sat weary.
Then I saw a mother and her babe,
A village woman she was,
The infant straddling her hip.
And there I saw what perhaps is God.
See the mothers that are.
They give birth to sons,
Are proud and jealous for them.
But when the sons leave
What can the mother do?
Except that God knows what is to be.

Poet: What do you mean by that?
Your words lack coherence.

Sadhu: Yes, they do, perhaps.
So long withdrawn from the world of men
I have lost the language whereby to tell you
What I mean. And again I scarcely know it

Myself, except that as I looked on the mother
And her babe I felt something shooting thro
Flooding my mind with Light.
As the world is darker after lightning
So am I.

*The Dacoit, who has been sharpening his knife on a stone, rises.*

Dacoit: Since she has taken refuge here
Here behind you, stalwarts ha?
I will go and

Chorus: Go Godless one, go.

Nun: Go, heathen, leave us.

Zohra: Go, wanderer, and if you come across a grave
Fresh dug, do not step on it I pray.

Dacoit: And so with one voice you dismiss me,
You who so fanatically kill each other
For your faiths, slaughter women and children
Where I but steal their gold. (*Exit.*)

Chorus: There he goes. But what footsteps are these?
Whose anklet bells do we hear?

*Enter, from left, Prem Behn—a Punjabi woman of thirty-six. She wears a six-yard pale pink cotton sari dotted with fine hand-embroidered flowers.*

Prem Behn: From the plains, the green land
Which once embraced the five rivers, I come
To see this renowned vale where my son is fighting now.
Long I travelled, on to Jammu had I been
From where he last wrote me.
They say one should come up the Jhelum valley
To see Kashmir slowly unravelling before one's eyes—

The panoramic view as we emerge out of the valley
Down which the Jhelum roars in youthful abandon.
But I came from Jammu. Dull was the road, I thought,
Till out of the tunnel we zoomed—and then
The magic beauty overpowered me. Out of the darkness
I came into the light and there far below
Lay the vale of Kashmir, like some wonderland
Of our dreams, encircled by high mountains
That guard it jealously.
Oh Kashmir, Kashmir, valley beloved of gods,
Who would not love thee at sight?
The green vale where flowers in such profusion bloom
As are never elsewhere seen. The Valley of Flowers!
Surely Parvati stepped this way to meet her Lord
And flowers opened out instantly!
Surely this is the abode of gods.
See the eternal snows rear their proud peaks
And kiss the sky!

Oh Kashmir, what forms thy beauty takes!
Now like an apsara divine, far above human desire,
You open your green fields and singing streams.
Now with masculine strength appear
(your impregnable heights,)
Glaciers, wild torrents, landslides,
And far above is the snowline
Pure undefiled home of the Great Destroyer.
Oh Kashmir willingly I'll die for thee.
And if one life can help my motherland keep thee,
That life is ready here.

Proud am I that my son is fighting
For such a prize. Lovely vale, had I a hundred sons
I'd send them all to fight for thee, and consider it
Scant sacrifice for such a treasure.

Long I lived in the plains below

Not knowing I had heaven so near me.
This is heaven. This is Paradise.
This is the loveliest spot in the universe.
And since there needs must be Truth where Beauty is,
This is Truth.

On the rapture of this scene!

Dear land, fight for Kashmir.
Order your sons here. They may die
And deem themselves fortunate.
India, my India, freely I forgive you

*Backstage there is a scream of pain following a shot. A body thuds to the ground. Silence for a minute. Hari, a young Indian pilot, crawls in slowly, pistol in hand.*

Chorus: Who is this? all bloody and maimed
Crawling towards us in such pain?

Poet: A son of India who must die
Whose blood must flow in that stream I saw
Whose mother waits in the distant plain
And waits in vain. Mothers, bear no more sons
If you want to spare the pain that befalls you
And them; the carrions hasten their bleeding end
And you with hopeful hearts wait, and wait in vain.

Hari: That brigand, that viper who calls himself man
Tried to steal my pistol. . .
Thought I was too weak. . .
Two days beside my shattered plane
No water, bleeding, I choke. . .
Thank you pal.
Brings my tongue to life again.
That bloody bastard
Had a hope, he did, lousy bum,
That he could snitch it off me.

Look at him now.
Deader than a bitch.

Chorus: The bandit? In tight trousers, scarred face?

Hari: Maybe the same, maybe not. All bandits look alike.
Had a bloody razor stropping it on the stone
Cool as you please, son of a bitch.

Meenakshi: (*coming forward*) His voice!
His voice but so full of anger
So unlike the laughing tone
That rang through our home.

Hari: Amma!

Meenakshi: My son, my Hari. I have found you
At last. But O my son!

*She strokes his bristly face. She feels his limbs and as she strokes his left leg. . .*

Hari: Oh ma!

Meenakshi: Shot away? Broken?
Child, was it for this you came here?
So far from home. Dearest boy, O
If I could do something to ease your pain.

Hari: Nothing can be done, Amma
"Touched to the quick he said
I am killed sire, and smiling
With his chief beside, the boy fell dead."
Blimey, what a thing to remember
In one's last hour on earth!

Next I'll start prattling Jack and Jill.
Don't cover my mouth, Amma,
It *is* my last hour.

Chorus: Sons must die

Poet: And mothers wait in vain

Hari: But I feel
So secure back in your womb
I can enter the tomb of time
And hear the breakers evermore
Lashing down those castles of mine
With walls of shell and crab prints
To the very moat of Hereafter.
I think I am getting boozed up, ma,
Seeing you, your hands, your eyes
Your widowed forehead, was it long drawn?
His end?

Meenakshi: Tell me about yourself,
This war
This plane
Were you happy while you were

Hari: Few men realize their dreams fully
Few prayers are granted wholly. . .
Ma, when I was a boy
Playing cricket in the field
Behind our house
As twilight steeped the pitch
We would hear the Bombay plane.
The ball would snick off my unheeding bat
Or snipe the bails abroad
While I stood watching the two red lights
And twinkling green
Till they swam out of view.
And it was my nightly prayer
That one day I might pilot a plane
Into the sky
And touch the face of God.
Fly, fly high

This my prayer.
I have flown high
Seen this lovely land
And here I die.

Meenakshi: Did
you
touch
the face of God?

Hari: Switches, buttons, earphones, messages.
I could feel His breath kissing the wings
And I stretched my hand
Switches, buttons, earphones
But Amma!
I see divinity!

He looked through your eyes now
An all embracing love, understanding.
Amma, you have come far
But you have come to me
Is that not enough?

Chorus: A flash comes and fades.
Man ennobled is laid at the door
Of divinity.
Far have they travelled
But not in vain.

Hari: Amma, was ever place beautiful as this?

Meenakshi (*grudgingly*) It is beautiful
Hari: Ma, our sands stretched out beside the sea
Was more beautiful, was it not?
I see the white foam wall
The handscooped towers I built
For you.
And now for a moment I saw divinity gleam,

Let me close my eyes and see it again—
(*Dies*)

Prem Behn: A beautiful death.
To die for one's country,
With mother's tears to close his eyes. . .

Chorus: Dead and dying, mourners, bereaved,
O Kashmir, must your pure white be stained
With gore? What else is in store for you?

Calamity! those slow footsteps bode ill.
So it is. Two men, a stretcher, on it
A soldier wrapped in tricolor.
What brave end did you meet, soldier,
That you lie wrapped in the flag?

*Enter two men carrying a bier. They place the bier on the ground. They wipe their hands, cracking the knuckles and bending their fingers to ease the stiffness.*

Pall-bearer: Come, brother, let us rest awhile
Ere we continue our sad march.

Chorus: Ah me! a young man, his soft hair
Scarce sprouting on his chin. And here
His knapsack. Born eighth October
Nineteen twenty seven. So young!

Prem Behn: Eighth October? Twenty seven?

Chorus: Lieutenant Nand Kishore
Fifty sixth Punjab Infantry
Died in line of duty, February 6, 1948.

Prem Behn: Let me see him.
He, yes he!
Nand Kishore, my *ladla*, my son. . .
(*A rumble from the corpse.*)

Chorus: What is that?

Nand Kishore: I refuse to be dead.

Prem Behn: Kishori!

Nand Kishore: Is it my mother's voice I hear?

Prem Behn: Yes, my darling.

Nand Kishore: Mother, I do not wish to be dead.

Chorus: This passeth understanding.
Boy, why do you act thus?
Strange times, indeed,
That dead men speak.

Nand Kishore: More strange I would say
That a young man in perfect health
Should die in one fell second.
I refuse to be dead.
Death is for men whose life energy is sapped
With life's joys and sorrows.
Death is for those who have *lived.*
But I, just turned twenty mother, is it not?
Do you remember?

Prem: Child, can I forget
My firstborn's first touch upon my breast?

Nand: I am too young to be dead.
I refuse.
I want to live;
Feel the blood of youth coursing
Through my veins,
To race over the fields, to swim across the Sutlej,
To see Spring's first sprig,
To join harvest songs and dances,
To get the sting of winter's freezing cold,

To feel the sun upon my face.
And I want to laugh, mother.
I have not laughed since I left the Sutlej banks
That day I donned my uniform.
As I lay dying, pictures of my boyhood games
Passed before me and I tried to smile.
The parched lips cracked in protest.
Is it a sin to smile, mother?

Happy days. Marbles, kites, tops.
And then YOUTH
O the very memory will drive me
To life.
Mother, give me life once again. O ma
You can do it. You did it once.
Do so again. Give me life.
So warm to be alive
But now I am not alive
I am dead. No
I am not dead. I refuse to be so.
I am not alive.
My spirit wanders with the wind
Too young too young to die.

What right had they to kill me?
Kashmir, I risked my life for you
My dearest possession
My breath I have given for you.
Be noble, Kashmir.
As becomes a noble friend
Return my gift threefold.
Beautiful gem set in majesty
Return my life to me.
You do not hear, Kashmir.
Answer me, why don't you answer me?
You have claimed too many
Not to be held responsible,
Old men leave widows

And children to mourn their death. Let me live
That I may have sons to mourn mine,
That I may leave some part of me
Here on earth, my blood warm
In the veins of a son.
Answer me, Kashmir,
Answer me cowards all
Why am I not alive?

Prem: My son, stop, my son, my son.
You died for your country!

Nand: Country?
What do I care what happens to my country?
I asked nothing of it except to live.

Prem: Kishori, it has given you a hero's end.

Nand: But I never wanted to be a hero.
All I asked my land was to let me be
A common man, live a common life
Beside my sweet Sutlej.
I do not want to die.

Prem: All men must die, my child.
Go to the Infinite Silence.
All of us must die.

Nand: Yes, but not at twenty
Prem: Go, dearest child, go.

Nand: You, my mother, want me dead!

Prem: If with my life I could give you life, I would.
But since it cannot be, go rest, my child.

Nand: Rest? There is no rest for such as I.
We must ever waft with every wind:

Too young too young to die

Prem: You have done your duty. Go.

Nand: Was it my duty to die a dog's death?

Prem: Your duty to your land

Nand: India, once I loved you,
O so intensely I loved your fields
Your history, your heritage.
But you killed me
India now I

Prem: Don't say it, child, don't.
Go Kishori, go.

Nand: O mother, why do you push me away?
Are my limbs maimed? is my face so disfigured
You cannot bear the sight? Tell me, mother

Prem: My darling, a more perfect form there cannot be
And your face has the pulsing exuberance
That flowed in your warm blood.

Nand: Why then do you wish me gone?

Prem: What shall I say?
Few men, as he said, few men
Are granted, as he said,
Few men are blessed
To die at the fullest moment.
You are one.
Few die in so noble a cause.
You are one.
You were blessed
Blessed to die at the fullest.
Go, Kishori, go.

Poet: Take my life, friend, and live. (*Stabs himself*)
Take it, Allah, ha Allah!

Chorus: Ah me, the moon has struck him
And he lies dead in the stream of blood he saw,
O Kashmir, beloved vale, what is to be?
Could I but know what is to be

Nand: Mother. . .

Prem: Go.

Nand: (*pleadingly*) Mother. . .

Prem: (*wearily but intensely*) Go my son,
Dearer to me than life, go.

Nand: O mother. . .

Prem: I am left alone with only my ideals
To support me. Leave me my ideals,
Illusions if you will.
Leave me this poor bequest.
For I have yet to live
And live with love in my heart
Not hate.

Go my darling, go.

Nand: I go, mother. I don't know why
For I cannot understand you.
But the pleading in your voice
Comes straight to me and I know
I must go.

# MEERA
# A DANCE DRAMA

***CHARACTERS***

Krishna

Meera, (also Devaki, Yasoda, Radha)

Rana, attendants, and courtiers

Court Dancer

Children, Krishna, Gopis and others

Voices from above

## SCENE I

*The left centre of the stage, separated from the rest of the stage by a semi-circular backdrop of lush-green trees and flowering shrubs, is Meera's garden. Sunbeams filter through the leaves and play upon a black-marble statue of Krishna the Fluteplayer, occasionally reflecting flashes of silver from his dress, flute and armbands.*

*To the right rear is the Rana's pleasure palace. It is surrounded by red-sand soil and has neat rows of trees and shrubs of the cactus family. From its lighted rooms come distant sounds of music and coarse laughter. In the farther background, on a rocky hill, stands the fortress of Chittore.*

*As the Curtain rises, Meera is seen kneeling in front of Krishna's statue, washing his feet. She then puts tilaka on his forehead, decks him with garlands, makes her offering of fruits, flowers and milk. She picks up her tampura and sits beside Krishna, strumming the strings with the fingers of her right hand. In her left hand she holds a pair of cymbals.*

*A single spotlight is on her. The rest of the stage is dimly lit.*

**MEERA:** I am Meera, handmaid of Lord Krishna now and forever. I have sat thus many a happy day, singing the song of songs, the song of Krishna's life here on earth.

I live in the ever-present Now because Krishna dances in my heart, the dance of joy from which alone can spring love, laughter, every worthwhile thing. Men and women around me, trapped in the coils of time, talk endlessly, hoping to make me live as the world says a woman should live. But their voices seem to come from afar, remote and meaningless because my ears can hear only the sound of Krishna's flute as he plays in Brindavan.

They say I was born a princess and that I was wed to Prince Bhoj, heir to the throne of Chittore, and that I have been mad a long time, and that my kinsmen feel I have betrayed family honour by leaving the palace for this garden, and that—ah, what does it matter what they say? for I am Meera, handmaid of Lord Krishna now and forever.

But I remember many things as I sit here waiting for Krishna.

I remember the gentle Prince Bhoj who asked me for my hand and my heart, and to whom I gave all I could, which was not much. I remember he died a warrior's death and left his father and his people grieving.

His brother wears the crown now, the crown that has adorned the best and bravest of Rajput kings over the centuries. They say he makes a travesty of the Rajput code of royalty, the code of truth and honour, courage and compassion that his fathers followed.

They say he spends his days and nights in the company of courtesans and flatterers. They say he hates me. These and other things they say who hope to make me live as a princess should. But I say nothing of them or him for neither their world nor his world is my world.

*Meanwhile the centre right of the stage has gradually brightened and brought to the fore an ornately decorated hall of the Rana's palace. Court attendants have entered and announced the Rana who comes in, followed by several courtiers. The Rana has asked for the dancer who enters and dances her greetings.*

**MEERA:** But I remember gratefully that because of this man who now sits on the throne of Chittore, Krishna came into my very being and absorbed the cup of poison meant for me. Great was the suffering till Krishna came, but greater far the fulfilment when I felt my lord's soothing touch upon my burning breast. I can feel it even now—the suffering and the bliss.

*The light on Meera's garden fades and the rest of the stage is brightly illuminated. The dancer swirls round to sensual music. There is an obvious rivalry for the Rana's attention between the dancer and the women who stand behind him with fans, offering him drink and inviting his caresses.*

*The dance ends and the Rana dismisses the dancer with one of the many gold necklaces he is wearing.*

*He then calls for Meera whose garden now lights up. When Meera enters, the Rana makes an elaborate show of welcome and offers her a cup of wine. Meera holds the cup to her lips, lowers it, and then raises it again and drinks the wine with closed eyes. She falters back, writhes in agony and then is suddenly restored. She dances exultantly. The palace hall and its people fade away as she continues her dance.*

**MEERA:** *(with hands raised in rapturous celebration)* Yes, I quaffed off the poison and danced. The tyrant did not know that for my Krishna who sucked dry the poisoned breasts of the vampire-nurse sent by Kamsa, for my Krishna who killed the venomous serpent Kalinga, the cup of poison was as mere smouldering fire to the monsoon floods.

Sharp was the suffering, but keener far the bliss. What greater fulfilment is there in life than to have Krishna dancing within oneself, what greater joy than to sing of Him, Eternal Lover, Infinite Love?

And so I sing the song of songs, the song of Krishna's life here on earth.

And as I relive my Krishna's birth, I become Devaki who brought forth the Child Divine.

## SCENE II

*The stage is in complete darkness for a moment. When the lights come on, Meera, as Devaki, is at the other end of the stage, which is now a long, narrow dungeon. The sloping sill of the high recessed window at the centre shows the immense thickness of the stone walls. Dark clouds are visible through the iron grill of the window.*

*Devaki is on a bare wooden bench. Vasudeva walks back and forth behind her.*

**DEVAKI:** There was a time when, with no thought of the future, I danced along the halls of this very palace in whose darkest dungeon I now sit huddled, waiting with aching heart for the sword the dawn will bring. There was a time when my brother, he whom men call Kamsa the Tyrant, loved me as intensely as he hates me now.

I remember when that love turned to hate. It was on that day when Kamsa joyfully charioted my bridal carriage through the sunlit streets of Mathura. It was at the moment the voice from heaven ceased, the voice that said, "Lo! the tyrant's rule shall end at the hands of Devaki's eighth child and He shall be the light of the world."

Straightaway Kamsa drove back to his palace and cast us into this cell. And here we have lived, my gentle lord and I, and here on this wooden bed have I panted in travail seven times and brought forth seven fair infants, all but one slain by the tyrant whom fear and passing Time have made more oppressive.

And now, on the eighth night of the waning moon in August, I lie once more, waiting. Is it a birth I wait for, or is it death?

*The rumble of the storm that has started meanwhile now grows louder. Through the high opening can be seen lightning flashes and driving rain.*

**DEVAKI:** Oh the anguish and the ecstasy of birth! Pain, oh blissful pain! Oh joy of life and light.

*The Child is born. Vasudeva picks Him up by the heels, washes Him and lays Him by Devaki's side.*

**DEVAKI:** My child, helpless, adorable.

Joy did I say? Ah me, the night recedes, and every moment brings the tyrant's sword closer to my babe. Stay! clouds, stay still in the firmament. Time! Stand still!

**VOICE FROM ABOVE:** Vasudeva, rise and take this Child across the river to the hut of Nanda, cowherd chief of Gokula, and bring away the girl child that has been born to Yasoda this night.

*Vasudeva, perplexed but obedient, carries away the Child through the door that opens automatically. Devaki, limp with pain and sorrow, weeps.*

*Soon Vasudeva returns. Seeing he is carrying a child, Devaki greets him joyously.*

**DEVAKI:** My child, my own sweet one. *(Is about to take the child but notices it is not hers and turns away.)* No, not mine, Where is he? Where did you leave him? Oh-h-h!

*The child cries. Vasudeva persuades her to take it but she refuses. Vasudeva reasons with her. A child is always heaven-sent, no matter who begets and who bears it. But Devaki is inconsolable.*

*The clouds have cleared away and dawn approaches.*

*Steps and Kamsa's voice are heard as the huge wooden door is pushed open. Devaki rushes to the child and clasps it to her bosom in an agony of love.*

**KAMSA'S VOICE:** Open the door and let me see for myself that it is a girl.

**VOICE FROM ABOVE:** *(As the stage is plunged in darkness)* Kamsa! thy destroyer lives in a village across the river, and he will come here as foretold.

## SCENE III

*Meera is back in her alcove. The spotlight is on her, while the rest of the stage is dim.*

**MEERA:** What greater fulfilment is there than to have Krishna dancing in one's heart, what greater joy than to sing of Him, Eternal Lover, Infinite Love?

And as I relive my Krishna's childhood in the village of Brindavan by the banks of the Yamuna, I see him at his boyish pranks, now playing hide-and-seek, now teasing the *gopis*, now stealing butter and mischievously protesting his innocence as children do. And I become Yasoda, fond foster-mother who thought her child a child as any other until that day she saw the universe contained within him.

*The rest of the stage lights up to show a village fore-ground. Children, led by Krishna, troop in, play ball and then steal butter from earthen pots hung from the ceiling. As Krishna pulls at the second pot, it breaks and the butter is spilled on the ground. Krishna and his companions scoop up the butter along with mud and stuff it into their mouths. They run and hide as Yasoda (Meera) comes in from the right. She catches several of them and reprimands them as she wipes their faces. She then searches for Krishna and pulls him out of his hiding place. She spanks him on his hands and bottom when he refuses to let her wipe his face. At last she succeeds in opening his mouth to clean it of the mud. In his mouth she sees the universe and swoons away.*

## SCENE IV

*Meera is in her alcove, in exactly the same pose in which she had been as Yasoda. Slowly she recovers and sits up.*

**MEERA:** Ah! Yasoda, fond mother, for a moment, you beheld his divinity and then the veil of Maya descended on you once again, and he once more became a child as any other. But we who know the story of his life, know that he went on the Mathura and slew the tyrant Kamsa, and that he was counsellor to kings and that on the field of Kurukshetra where the Pandavas and the Kauravas were arrayed for battle, he Krishna, revealed himself to Arjuna as the total incarnation of Vishnu, Preserver of the Universe, come on earth to re-establish justice saying:

"Whenever there is decay of righteousness, O Arjuna, and there is exaltation of unrighteousness, then I Myself come forth.

For the protection of the good, for the destruction of evil-doers, for the sake of establishing justice, I am born from age to age."

Oh cosmic dancer who art the centre and circumference of the universe, womb of all being and seed of all existence, salutations to thee!

## SCENE V

*Krishna at centre stage is "frozen" in the same pose as in the marble statue.*

**MEERA:** I could gaze forever on the grace and beauty of that perfect form which entering me makes mine own more beautiful.

And as I gaze, veil upon veil is rent and I see the face of Truth. I see that Truth is ineffable and can only be expressed in symbols and myths.

*Krishna fades. There is a soft musical interlude in which the sitar slowly gives way to a distant flute that comes closer and closer. Meera starts speaking with the last notes of the musical interlude.*

**MEERA:** Symbols and myths
I perceive the truth of the love-play between the *gopis* and Krishna—it is the finite reaching out for the infinite, the *atman*, soul within, desiring to merge with the *Paramatman*, the soul above.

How rapturously they dance as they recall their afternoon with Krishna. How they dwell on the beauty of his perfect form, the circlet of peacock feathers around his lovely brow, the enchanting melody of his flute. . . .

*The gopis have come in one by one and now they dance, describing Krishna. Then they retreat to take positions at various household chores.*

**MEERA:** As I see the face of truth, I see that this love is our human longing for the divine. But the veil of Maya descends on me once more, and I know nothing but that I love; nor whence nor why but only that I love.

And I become Radha for whom each moment of waiting is an aeon of aching joy. And when I hear the sound of Krishna's step on the soft grass, my heart blossoms even as the petals of the sun-flower burst open when their lord comes riding out of night.

*The sound of the flute grows louder and Krishna enters as if from the statue. The gopis drop whatever they are doing and dance with him in joyous abandon. Soon he seems to tire of them, for he keeps looking out for someone. His face lights up when Radha [Meera] enters from the right. The group dance proceeds with fresh vigour. The gopis leave one by one. Then Radha and Krishna dance to the song of creation. As the dance ends, Krishna recedes into the statue and Radha becomes Meera kneeling at the feet of the marble Krishna.*

**CURTAIN**

# SITA'S PROMISE

***CHARACTERS***

Narrator

Lakshmana

Rama

Sita

First Girl

Second Girl

Gypsy Queen

Valli

Dancers

*A behind-the screen projector and screen provide an 8'x15' back drop on which appear slides appropriate to each scene. Rama, Lakshmana and Sita move in a small area stage right. After their first entry they are on stage throughout the drama.*

*The dancers enter rear right and exit rear left. The spotlight on the actors dims with the beginning of each dance.*

*Curtain rises on dancers in position.*

**NARRATOR:** *(as the dancers do their namaskaram)* Glory to you, Lakshmi, you who hold the sanctified veena in your soft hands, lotus-eyed queen who has the unparalleled beauty of virtue, Consort of Vishnu, giver of boons, mother of lotus-seated Brahma, salutations to you.

*Invocation Dance "Vara Veena" followed by Alarippu.*

*Exit dancers*

## SCENE I

*The backdrop shows a forest with large-trunked trees. Two huts*

**NARRATOR:** Rama, Prince of Ayodhya, was banished for fourteen years by his father, Emperor Dasaratha, at the behest of his stepmother Kaikeyi who wanted the throne for her own son, Bharata. Rama left his father's kingdom, accompanied by his wife Sita and his brother Lakshmana.

Rama, Sita and Lakshmana travelled far and wide in the forests of India, always helping the wise and holy men who lived alone or in hermitages. The brave brothers fought against rakshasas, and killed or drove away demons who harassed the sages by interrupting their rituals and mediation.

Thus passed ten years. It was now the tenth month of the eleventh year. All the flowering trees were in full bloom, the red leaves of the flame-of-the-forest and the lingering fragrance of white parijata vying with the many shades of green that clothed the ancient forest of Dandakaranya.

*Rama and Lakshmana enter. Both are dressed as in typical representation-dhoti, quiver of arrows, bow on left shoulder. Lakshmana is carrying a bird.*

**LAKSHMANA:** *(smiling with boyish satisfaction)* My sister Sita will be so pleased with this!

**RAMA:** *(seriously)* Lakshmana, I sometimes worry that the two of you have not grown a whit in all these years. You are as playful as children. Our forest life is almost ending and in two years we must start on our return journey to take up our responsibilities in Ayodhya. I am afraid we—you and I and the sages and their students—all of us have pampered Sita.

**LAKSHMANA:** No more than our mothers and her friends would have.

**RAMA:** She is so innocent, so spontaneous in all her movements and responses, my heart fills with wonder and joy every day when I return home from my day's work. A girl-wife is a delight, brother, but a girl-queen?

A queen must have the majesty of Goddess Shakti, the compassion of Goddess Sri; she should be a mother to the highest and the lowliest . . .

**LAKSHMANA:** *(interrupting impatiently)* Rama, the daughters of King Janaka were born and reared to be queens no less than we were born and raised to be kings and warriors. When the time comes, we shall wear our crowns as naturally as we now wear our forest weeds, sire, *(He gives a sarcastic inflection to "sire.")*

*Sita comes out of her hut. She is in her twenties, but as Rama has said, she has the naivety of an unspoilt girl.*

**SITA:** *(delighted)* What a strange bird! This light blue, it reminds me of a still lake, look at the shades of blue under its wing!

**RAMA:** It is a water bird that flies over oceans.

**SITA:** What is it doing in an inland forest? Oh, look, you poor thing, you are hurt, I'll take care of you. *(She rushes into the hut. Rama and Lakshmana remove their bows and arrows. . .)*

## SCENE II

*Later that day. Same scene. Lakshmana is sharpening arrows. Rama is reclining against a tree. Sita is sorting berries. Hermitage girls come in.*

**FIRST GIRL:** Sita, you haven't come to our ashram for a whole week! Look at our new dance dress. Isn't it pretty?

**SITA:** They are gorgeous. Are you going to dance for me?

**SECOND GIRL:** Yes, this is our newest dance.

*The girls dance Jatiswaram*

**SITA:** *(embracing the younger ones)* That was lovely, girls. You have improved so much. Remember how careless you were at first about keeping your elbows up and bending your knees?

*She embraces each as they run away*

**LAKSHMANA:** We have been here a long time. When we first came, Aparna was hardly out of her baby lisp. Look how she has grown! Do you have any plans for moving on, brother? or should I start re-roofing my hut?

**RAMA:**It is so peaceful here.

**SITA:** Too peaceful, Rama.

**LAKSHMANA:** All the demons have been destroyed. There is nothing to do. Let's go elsewhere.

**SITA:** You said we should visit sage Agastya before we return.

**RAMA:** Yes, soon we should be thinking of our return; it is not a happy thought.

**SITA:** I don't at all look forward to all that noise and worry. Any time is too soon, Rama, the years have flown by too too soon.

**RAMA:** *(laughing indulgently)* How soon you change your song, Sita. Just a moment ago you said this is too peaceful. Now you say Ayodhya is too busy and noisy.

**SITA:** How like you, my Rama, to see only two options. Can't I be bored with our routine here and still not look forward to the duties that await us? Can't I long for something else, to see the world? We don't have much time and there is so much to see, so many lands, so many peoples, so many skies, so many birds. Oh Lakshmana, tell me about this bird!

**LAKSHMANA:** My brother is better versed in such knowledge.

**RAMA:** It is a tern, Sita, an Arctic tern that divides its time between the north and south poles, making this flight of twice ten thousand miles every year. Its kind is never seen in this country for its path is always above and around the countries of the far, far west. Its destination now is the primeval ocean where Lord Vishnu reposes on Snake Adisesha.

**LAKSHMANA:** If we could learn the language of birds, we could know a lot more of the skies and lands you long to see, sister.

**SITA:** Hear how clearly she speaks to us through her eyes, her fluttering wings, her beating heart! Poor, lonely, lost little stranger, come make this your home. *(The bird wails.)*

**LAKSHMANA:** It wants to go home. Why not we take it back to its home?

**SITA:** *(thrilled)* Yes, yes, let's. Rama, oh please let's do that!

**RAMA:** Even had we the wings of an eagle, it would take us two months to fly there.

**SITA:** But we do have wings. The king of eagles, Jatayu himself, will carry us.

**RAMA:** Jatayu is visiting Himavan. Besides, all this is foolish. We do not have the time. We must visit Sage Agastya; perhaps the hermits in the southern forests need our help, and then it would be time to return. Our subjects are waiting for us.

**SITA:** Once we return, we shall never be able to get away.

**RAMA:** I am no more enthusiastic about returning to Ayodhya than you, Sita; we have been so happy here. But duty calls us.

## SCENE III

*Next day. Rama and Lakshmana come in from their day's work. Sita runs out of her hut and greets them.*

**SITA:** I have news for you, brother. I met a gypsy queen this morning. She gave me an ointment for our little bird. She wanted to dance for me with her friends *(sound of music)* Oh, they are here already! What are they singing? The music is so lively.

**LAKSHMANA:** *(goes to the edge of stage and listens)* They are describing the beauties of their native hills which are graced by temples of Siva and Subrahmanya. And of course, they are making the usual fantastic claims about love potions and herbs that would make kings your slaves and have everyone faint for love of you. They say that they weave baskets and threshing trays for their living, and that we should give them grain in exchange for their fortune-telling. They say their fortune-telling is never wrong.

*Kurathi/Gypsy dance*

**SITA:** Thank you, sisters, many thanks. Stay and teach me how to float on waves of music as you do, how to be so happy and carefree. But first, let me give you something to eat and drink.

**GYPSY QUEEN:** We have brought some rare fruits and flowers for you. In a minute we'll bring them in.

*All the gypsies leave*

**SITA:** She looks so full of vitality and confidence. I shall have her read my fortune.

**RAMA:** *(sternly)* No, Sita, no. Be hospitable and kind by all means, but you shall not have your palm read.

**SITA:** *(disappointed)* It would be fun to know what the future holds for us.

**RAMA:** No, dearest, it is not for man to know his future. Man has been given memory so he can learn from the past, but he has not been given eyes to see into the future because it is best he accepts each day as it comes, that he works with hope and prayer, not with some knowledge that would make him laze or despair.

## SCENE IV

*Next day, afternoon. The three are on top of a hill.*

**LAKSHMANA:** Here we are, on the peak at last.

**SITA:** Why did we climb up this steep hill?

**RAMA:** Because it is here. It is human nature to climb every high hill one sees, to swim every deep river one comes across. There is something in us that drives us to undertake more than seems possible.

**SITA:** *(teasingly)* Like the something that makes us want to know the future?

**RAMA:** You are still tempted by the gypsy's boasts, Sita. Do not seek to know what is to be. What if the future holds sadness? Would you rather be as you are, ignorant and trusting, or would you rather suffer like Savitri, knowing all along she would be widowed a year from her wedding day?

**SITA:** That is a thought too terrible to bear. I don't have that kind of strength.

**LAKSHMANA:** The daughters of Janaka were born and raised to be queens and they have always, and will always, act with the strength expected of superior beings.

**SITA:** *(busy in her own imagining)* I have had the power! It must be somewhere within, unused. For I remember now. The moment I saw you, Rama, in Father's Great Hall of the Bows, I saw myself placing the bridal garland of pink roses around your neck.

**RAMA:** *(laughing)* And I saw myself stringing Siva's bow the moment I saw you, my lovely princess, on your balcony as I walked into your father's palace. But that was wishful thinking, not a vision!

**LAKSHMANA:** *(gently)* Sister, God places His hand on our head for brief moments and we do see visions. That is one of the many blessings of being human.

**RAMA:** But only God can see steadily into the future, for He alone is Lord of Time. For the rest of us. . . .

**SITA:** *(interrupting)* What's Time? This mysterious Time that makes a day seem a year when you are away, and a year a day when you're near?

**RAMA:** *(thoughtfully)* I do not know Sita. I only know there are at least two levels of awareness—the human and the divine. It is like us sitting in this grove—we can see only the trees around us but someone who is perched on a cloud can see the whole hill and to someone who is way above the earth, the hills and plains and forest and sea are all laid out flat—the past and present and future all come together as the Eternal Present. As Lakshmana says, if the veil of Maya is ever lifted from us, we shall see as God sees for we shall be in Eternity, in the Everlasting Now.

**SITA:** The sages whose yogic power gives a glow to these forests, who wear knowledge as lightly as you wear your bow, can they lift the veil of Maya?

**RAMA:** I suppose so. Yes, Yoga can train us to reach that spiritual level just as pursuit of material knowledge continually expands man's physical control of Nature. But only God, who perpetually exists beyond Time, can lift the veil of Maya for us ordinary beings.

*As they walk, the lights shimmer and flash, denoting a vision. A girl in dim darkness is on the floor.*

**SITA:** Oh, poor girl, she is so beautiful and so sad!

**RAMA:** She is intoxicated.

**SITA:** *(shocked)* Rama! what a thing to say! Look at her eyes, so lovely, so desperate, and yet there is a glow.

**RAMA:** Let us turn back. We have a long way to go.

**SITA:** Let's talk to her. *(Music and words of Varnam)*

**RAMA:** *(sternly)* Leave her alone. She is half mad. Such open lamentations and declarations of love are *(he shrugs contemptuously)*

**SITA:** How harsh you are, Rama. She is saying, "Even if the whole world is destroyed I shall not forget you." She thinks she is alone, poor girl. Let us show ourselves.

**RAMA:** Alone or in company, my love, one should not make such an open display of one's emotions. Self-control is a cardinal virtue.

*The girl rises and takes a dance pose*

**SITA:** *(as words come on)* Listen to her. She says it is no secret that she is desperate for him. For whom? Why! She is in love with Lord Vishnu!

**LAKSHMANA:** *(softly)* She is all human souls crying in anguish at being separated from God!

*Varnam "Sakiye" Dance. Girl leaves.*

**SITA:** Some of the stories she sings about I know, but not the others. Brother, who is Balagopala? Who is Panchali whose honour he saved?

**LAKSHMANA:** *(laughing)* Maybe she was looking into the future.

**SITA:** *(also laughing)* Oh, you are teasing me! Maybe *she* is from the future and we were looking at something that hasn't happened yet!

*She claps her hands like a little girl who has won a point.*

**RAMA:** Let us go.

**LAKSHMANA:** *(with an inflection of sarcasm)* Our noble brother is not amused.

**RAMA:** Even if that poor woman is the human soul, it is weakness to let emotions rule instead of reason, to let desire rule instead of duty.

**LAKSHMANA:** *(angrily)* Oh, you talk by the book, Rama. Always by the book. Everything you do, you do because it is your **duty**—not because you enjoy it, not for itself. You help the hermits not because you admire their renunciation, but because it is your duty; you risk your life fighting demons not because you are angry at their vileness but because of duty; you love your wife not because she is so lovely, so pure, so devoted, but because it is your duty. If your book ever told you she was impure, you'd act by the book and abandon her though every beat of your heart, every nerve in your body cried out in protest. Oh Rama, Rama, who are you to preach, you who have never felt temptation or the sorrows of separation, never felt torn between love and duty?

**RAMA:** *(patronizingly)* Where love conflicts with duty, it must be made to give way, brother, for Duty must always, but always, come first. But you know it already, Lakshmana; you have done your duty, forsaking the pleasures of the palace for service in the forest.

**LAKSHMANA:** *(passionately)* No Rama. It was not my sense of duty but my love for you. **Love.** My duty was to my mother and yours who of a sudden were left childless; my duty was to my father, who might have lived had I been there to comfort him; my duty was to my wife, whose youth I have abandoned to fade and wilt in solitude and barrenness. What can you know of the soul's anguish or the body's hungers, my **noble** brother, you whom God has blessed with His perpetual presence and your wife's?

*He walks out.*

**SITA:** *(kneeling as to intercede)* My brother is still as impetuous as a boy, my Lord. Our life has been so sheltered here in the arms of Nature where black is black and white is white, here where the forests have been sanctified by the yogic power of sages and the innocence of hermitage children, that we have not gone through the sufferings and pain necessary for one to grow, to mature.

**RAMA:** *(who has raised her as she speaks, now falls on his knees before and speaks humbly)* Oh, Sita, all he says is so true. I **am** ignorant and conceited. The sages have given me so much knowledge but the little wisdom I have received, I have received from you and him. *(in anguish)* Oh God, if only I could be as sure as Lakshmana that when the time comes I shall not fail the royal house of Raghu.

*He bows in silence, then gets up and says in his normal voice*

My love, we shall start tomorrow and take your little bird to its home in the far north, where Dhruva the star of the Pole stands overhead. May the Supreme One be with us in our journey through space and time.

## SCENE V

*The scene is Brindavan—peacocks, cows, gopis.*

**NARRATOR:** They journeyed northward and in time came to Brindavan where in later days would be born Krishna, total incarnation of Lord Vishnu. And the veil of Maya was lifted once more for them and they were in the Everlasting Now where Krishna the divine fluteplayer eternally dances with the gopis, who so loved him that he appeared to each of them all at the same time, as a human being to touch and to hold.

*Back screen shows Krishna Leela*

**RAMA:** Look at the white flowers that bed the fields and banks by the river Yamuna. This is sacred soil, Sita, these small flowers grow where divinity breathes.

*The sound of girls' ghunghurus is heard. Sita listens.*

**SITA:** They seem to be complaining about someone!
**LAKSHMANA:** They are saying, is it fair of you to hide our clothes when we are bathing in the river? Is it fair of you to steal milk and butter from our huts when we are away at work? Is it fair to tease us with your mischief and tempt us with your caressing flattery?
**SITA:** They seem to like it anyway!

*Sabdam—Surasijakchulu—Dance*

*The girls leave after the dance and the three, who have been unseen, now come back on stage.*

**SITA:** There wasn't a trace of jealousy in them. This person with whom they are in love, he must be a king among men. They made him out to be an incarnation of Vishnu himself.

**RAMA:** Either they are seeing their human lover as a god, or God as a human lover. But when you think on it, maybe love is essentially the same. We express it differently to different persons—from mother to child to friend to lover. And God is all these and more, but our finite human perceptions can understand him only through human relationships.

**LAKSHMANA:** *(exaggeratedly)* Is it Rama who speaks thus? Wonders will never cease. My stuffy, pedagogical preachy brother has at last understood man's essential humanity. One of these days he might even see man's essential divinity, that we are all God within.

**RAMA:** *(good humouredly)* I may be a slow learner, my quick-witted Lakshmana, but don't give up on me.

## SCENE VI

*Mountains in the background.*

*Rama, Sita and Lakshmana enter. A peacock appears on the screen and runs out. A girl comes in a moment after it exits.*

**RAMA:** Tell me, sweet maid, the way to King Himavan's summer palace.

**GIRL:** If you'd tell me which way my Lord Muraga took. I saw his peacock a moment ago. *(To Sita)* Would you call him to me? Please. Tell him Valli is waiting.

**SITA:** I shall try to find him if you'd tell me whom to look for.

**VALLI:** Don't you know my Lord Muraga who rides on the dancing peacock? the brother of elephant-headed Ganesa? Don't you know Muraga who is Satgurunathan the Supreme Teacher of Ultimate Truth, he who imprisoned Brahma for misleading him, and then on finding Truth gave a discourse to his father Lord Siva?

*Sabdam—"Aadum mayil mel"—Dance*

**RAMA:** I think I know which path he took. Come, Valli, I'll take you a little way until you are out of this wood.

*Exit Rama and Valli*

**SITA:** Of late, Rama has become so much more considerate of human . . . failings *(She says the last word after a pause)*

**LAKSHMANA:** You don't really believe it is a weakness to feel, do you? to laugh, to cry, to shout and dance, even to get angry—these are not weaknesses, Sita.

**SITA:** Mankind is weak, aren't we?

**LAKSHMANA:** *(intensely)* Man is divine, Sita, and you know that as well as I do. Look at the works of humankind—our temples silhouetted against the dawn, our gardens and golden fields carved out of forests and deserts, our poets who have touched the face of God, oh how can any seeing, feeling, touching merely human being doubt the divinity of the fire within us? *(Pauses, and then in his normal voice)* The breeze is cold. Tomorrow I shall go hunting, sister. I shall get you a tigerskin to keep you warm.

**SITA:** Have you lost faith in me, Lakshmana?

**LAKSHMANA:** *(shocked)* What?

**SITA:** *(laughing)* The daughters of Janaka would surely have enough fortitude to withstand this cold.

**LAKSHMANA:** *(wistfully)* The daughter of Janaka would love this scene. The majesty of the mountains, the lash of the breeze, the tingling needles of water from the falls where we bathed this morning.

**SITA:** *(moved to tears)* Lakshmana, we've never spoken about such things in all these years, and I don't know where to begin. But often, oh so often, I have felt sad and guilty that I have my whole world with me and my sister has nothing at all.

**LAKSHMANA:** Don't feel guilty, Sita. Urmila and I have all that anyone needs. The hand of God is often upon us, and we see and feel each other more often than we deserve. In my dreams she comes to me, Sita, and dreams are often more real and satisfying than actual sight and touch. As Sri is to Narayana, as Shakti is to Siva is Urmila to me. Without her I am nothing. At times I feel strength surging through my body and I know then that she is thinking of me, praying for me, reaching out in spirit and embracing me. If I act like a god, it is because her love makes me one.

**SITA:** I feel humble, my brother, so profound are your experience and words. You should have gone with Valli for you **know** what she is talking about. You have been where the dance is.

**LAKSHMANA:** I can only say **there** I have been, but I cannot say where. And I cannot say for how long, for that is to place it in time.

**SITA:** Lakshmana, will I ever understand your words? Are we not in Time? Such strange people we have met, I wonder where we are. I don't understand.

**LAKSHMANA:** All you need to understand, Sita, is that if with my life I can prevent either of you from knowing the anguish of separation from each other or from God, I shall gladly do so. What I said with sarcasm the other day, I say with sincerity over again: My brother is blessed above all humankind with God's perpetual presence within him.

## SCENE VII

*Mountains*

**NARRATOR:** They climbed higher and were welcomed by King Himavan who escorted them still higher saying, "I must leave you for now, my friends; but here are the slopes of Parvati's sacred land. All creatures here, babe and beast and bird, sing of Siva in innocent abandon. Even the smallest child knows and imitates him who bears the sacred drum, who wears the skin of the tiger he killed barehanded, who dances for the delight of the sages. See, here come several children."

*Rama, Sita and Lakshmana have entered. Dancers enter. Natesa Kavuthuvam Dance*

## SCENE VIII

**RAMA:** This is the grove to which Himavan directed us. Jatayu will be here this evening.

**LAKSHMANA:** Here in the month of January, when the sun is in Jupiter, at noon, Siva will keep the promise that he made to the sages long ago and he will dance in this golden hall of Tillai to the worship of all creation. For what greater blessing can any mortal ask than to see Siva of arched eyebrows and waving hair raising his divine foot in cosmic dance?

**SITA:** I see no hall, no temple.

**RAMA:** It may be that Tillai the eternal city is the heart of Man. The golden roof and jewelled pillars will rise to reach of us when the time comes. Maybe it is a promise he had made to each one that he will dance in our heart, infinite flux in eternal harmony, circled by a ring of fire.

*The temple comes on the screen as he speaks and Siva in Nataraja pose appears; and they gaze in wonder*

*"Natanam adinar" Dance*

## SCENE IX

**NARRATOR:** Jatayu, the sacred eagle, carried the three travellers to the shores of the primeval ocean that we call Lake Agassiz. There they were welcomed by the people of that land. And the bird that Sita had carried so carefully through their journey was home at last.

*Slide shows a flock of Arctic terns. Sita enters, surrounded by Native children who dance for her*

*First Nations Dance*

## SCENE X

**NARRATOR:** And they wandered along the shores of Agassiz, loving and loved by the people. And then one day they wandered far away; and from the still point of the turning world rose Adisesha, the snake of primeval existence

*Slide of Vishnu slowly appears on the screen*

on whose ancient coils lay Lord Vishnu.

*All three gasp at the majestic sight of the Lord. They do a dance namaskaram and stay kneeling.*

**RAMA:** Narayana! Supreme Essence!
**VISHNU'S VOICE:** Rise, my son, I am well pleased with you.

*Rama continues to kneel*

Why, Rama, my own dear child, you gasp and keep your distance as though you don't know me, Me whose essence you bear.

**RAMA:** Father!
**VISHNU'S VOICE:** My beloved son.
**RAMA:** All my days and nights have led to this moment, this beatific moment. Narayana Narayana! Now I am ready to die for this is life everlasting.
**VISHNU'S VOICE:** *(laughing)* You are too earnest, my child. Why, you have hardly started your life.
**RAMA:** What greater bliss than to kneel here forever, Lord!
**VISHNU'S VOICE:** Not yet eternity for you, Rama. It is now time to return to Dandakaranya and make that visit to Sage Agastya.
**RAMA** :*(rising reluctantly)* If such is your will, my father.

## SCENE XI

*Sita comes in, surrounded by Native children*

**A CHILD:** You are the daughter of Manitou, aren't you?

**ANOTHER:** Of course she is. Can't you see how flowers grow wherever she walks?

**FIRST CHILD:** Make us more flowers, more grass, more monkeys, more of everything you told us about.

**SITA:** Oh, my little ones, I wish I could. But I am not a daughter of Manitou, or rather, I am only as much a child of the Great Spirit as any of you.

**CHILD:** How do flowers grow then, where you walk?

*Rama and Lakshmana enter*

**SITA:** For a short time I stood on holy ground. *(embracing a child)* I wish I could give you the beauty of our forests, our rivers, our elephants and our many coloured birds, and our warm sunshine.

**CHILD:** That's okay, Sita. We love you for yourself. Please stay.

**SITA:** How I wish I could stay with you in this lovely land.

**CHILD:** If you must go, promise you will come back to us.

**SITA:** I promise that, children. I shall come again to this lovely land of lakes and blue skies and snow. I, through my people, shall surely come again and we shall build our temple and sing our songs with all the children of all the different lands who make this their home. *(Todiya Mangalam—Jaya Janaki Ramana—Dance by ensemble)*

## CURTAIN

**Note.** *The translations of the main words of each song are incorporated into the script, and precede each dance so as to inform an audience, unfamiliar with the language and the dance form, about the story line.*

*This play was first staged in April 1981 at the Winnipeg Art Gallery.*

# DEAR DEEDI, MY SISTER

*At stage right is a section of an L-shaped living room of a middle-class home in Winnipeg.*

*Sapna, a woman from India, in her late twenties, dressed in a silk saree, is seated at the dining table. Behind her is a patio door through which can be seen a snow-covered yard with a row of evergreens at the far end. To her right is a wall unit of open teak shelves on which are some books, several decorative pieces, and a bronze figurine of Nataraja, god of dance. Near the bronze is an incense-stick stand with two lighted agarbatties. Sapna has a pen in hand, and there is stationery—letter pad, envelopes and stamps—on the table. A bowl of flowers that normally would have been at the centre has been pushed to the side of the table to make room for the stationery.*

**SAPNA:** Dear Deedi, my sister,
I haven't heard from you for a long time. When I first came, the mailman's daily visit was my lifeline. Even now, I wait by the window, whiling the hour away thinking of all of you back home. The breeze is lazily blowing fine snow across the front yard that is already buried under two feet of white. Nature, here as at home as I often say, is both bounteous and tyrannical. Wheat grows almost by itself, miles and miles of prairie gold; but now the fields are cold, dear God, it is so cold. I shall never get used to these needle pines that stand green against the white. For though the land around me is cedar and fir, in the landscape of my memory, there are other smells and sounds—of mango blossoms, monsoon rains, temple bells.

*Sound of temple bells*

Temple bells. I long to hear them, dear Deedi. I long to walk to our temple bearing flowers and incense for Parameswara, supreme lord of all.

*Sapna rises and dances an invocatory hymn to Nataraja Parameswara. She resumes her seat, and the spotlight picks up in turn each of the following speakers on stage left.*

**MARIELLA** (*a young woman from Nicaragua*):

Puerto Cabezas! I love you.
Your broad beach road where the polished tar
Flings mirages that vapour on the speeding cars,
Your sands stretched out beside the sea
Where at my feet laps Eternity.
Your sullen sky, your sweltering air,
Your flashy rich, the blind beggar's stare,
Wreck of thirty ruinous years
When the sheep looked up and were not fed.
Puerto Cabezas, I hope one day to call me your own
Though pledged now to the land
Which my love has made our home.

**WAMAHU** (*a young woman from Kenya*):

Under a sky more vast than any I've seen,
On snow more cold than ever I dreamed,
I stand alone
Amid masks that speak an alien tongue.

Far far those I loved and love
And far the fragrance of my native flowers
O'er which bees murmur homeland tunes.

**ILAGO** (*a little boy from the Philippines, playing with crayons on the floor*):

Ina, I like school.
It is such fun.
We play most of the time
And sing songs in French.
Ina, finger-painting is such fun!

So many bright bright colours
And we can use all we want.
Ina, if a crayon breaks
You can just throw it away
And take a new one!
Ma, you think you could change my name
To Jim, or David, or something?
Ina, I love recess time.
Did you see the tyres?
The tyres tied together?
And you can climb up and sit inside and swing!
Such fun.
When the snow comes, Ma,
I'll get less brown, won't I?
It would be nice to be white,
        more like everyone else
        you know?
I can do everything on the jungle-gym
That Petey can. I'll show you Saturday.
No school on Saturdays.
Just think, Ina, no school
Ever on Saturdays!
Except that it isn't so good
When you like school, you know?

**SEKONI** (*a young man from Nigeria, seated in a bus*):
Who are these faceless people
among whom my life is oozing away?
each is so self-assured,
        glancing swiftly but completely
        through me, wordlessly asking:
        Why are you here?
And the bus moves on, and we.

**NAYANA** (*a young woman from Gujarat, India, against a kitchen counter of an apartment*):
Namaste! Chandri Deedi, come in.
So good you are, Deedi,

looking me up so often
if all is well.
Seat your good self.
Yes, we got vacuum cleaner,
It is so convenient, no?
You phoned yesterday? O I am so sorry
I was not being here.
I will tell you the story, Deedi,
but first seat your good self.
There, I've put off stove. Let us sit.
It happened this way.
That good lady in next flat
she was going to food store
the Italian one, no? on the big street
and our Indian one so close
so I am also going.
I buy some vegetables, bhindi, and fresh brinjals,
and then I go to join her at her store.
The stink hits my nose, but I keep my face
from showing, no?
And then I look for her.
Toba, toba, Deedi, whole hunks
of animals hanging from hook
like we hang bananas, no?
Ram re Ram, my stomach churns
and I rush out.
You too laughing, Chandri Deedi?
He too is laughing when I tell him.
I have a lot to learn he is telling.
Let me boil some tea, yes, yes, Deedi, you must.
You are so kind, no?
like my own cousin sister you are being.
But is hard for me to speak English.

**AZIZA** (*an older woman from Pakistan, in a salwar suit*):
What kind of place you've brought me to, son?
Where the windows are always closed
and the front door it is always locked?

Son, son, it gives me great joy
to see you so well settled,
children and wife and all
Though my hairs do stand on end
when your wife hold hands with men
and you with other men's wives.
But I am glad son, I really am
that you are settled good good
and thought to bring me all the way
to see this lovely house and car and all.
But I cannot breathe this stale air
with yesterday's cooking smells
going round and round.
Son, cooking is an everyday thing
not a Sunday work alone.
And son, cooking should smell good.
The leaping aromas
    of turmeric and cumin,
    and mustard seeds popped in hot oil
that flavour food, not stink up the air.

Open the windows, son.
I am too used to the sounds
    of living things.
Of birds in the morning
Of rain and wind at night,
Not the drone of furnace fan
and hiss of hot blasts from vent
and whoosh whoosh of washing machine.

Open the windows, son,
and let me go back
    to sun and air
    and sweat and even flies and all
But not this, not this.

**CHOI CHAN** (*a middle-aged man from Hong Kong*):
Small comfort I find in these thorny spruce

That grow bleak against this white.
Where's the fire that can sustain us
In this alien land of endless skies?
Where the friend who'll lend a hand
So we stand tall in our own eyes?

**SAPNA:** [*goes to front door*] A letter at last!
But how heavy the news it brings!

*Throws the sheets down and sinks to the floor to mime and recite the following, as though reading from the letter*

It is hot, hot, always hot, and by noon I am exhausted. Cooking, cleaning, attending on the children, the menfolk, the parents-in-law. There are no servants to be had anymore. They prefer to work in weaving mills, garment factories, construction sites. . . . The water in the well is very low and the electric pump cannot be used. So we spend hours drawing water . . . there are welts on my palms and my shoulders ache. But these are hardships one can bear, for Nature, as you say, is sometimes bounteous and sometimes stingy as a mother-in-law. You envied me for marrying into a large family, saying I'd never want for company, Company I have, and in plenty—sisters-in-law, nephews, nieces, relatives, and of course, mother-in-law. It is her cruelty that is most hard to bear. Charu—you remember my letter about how fabulously showy my youngest brother-in-law's recent wedding was? Charu comes from a very rich house, and it has been misery for all of us since she came. Mother-in-law has started picking on me and Lakshmi again for not having brought as much dowry. But she does not spare Charu either, though Charu's dowry is much bigger than all of ours put together. Charu's father, she says, can afford a lot. True he can, and she is bent on squeezing him dry. If he does not come up with a colour television and more jewellery by Diwali, I am afraid for Charu. Sapna, my sister, you are lucky to be far away from all these burdens that womankind must bear in this our ancient land. Be happy in your new home. . . [*stops mime*]

Dear Deedi, my sister, what can I say?
Why must womankind bear such burdens? Why? As you say, I

am lucky. But not because I live here, my sister, but because my husband is so good and his family back home so kind. Here too women suffer, dear Deedi, for being women. The burdens are different but the pain is the same.

**CHANDRI** (*a woman from Sri Lanka*):

Twenty hours a week, I thought,
was surely something I should give
my people
now that the children
are at school all day.
It was satisfying at first
to drive back and forth.
Shop for apartment, furniture,
kitchen things, winter clothes;
a wooden stake and stocking bands
to withstand the first winter's winds.

Lovely the clematis
Against our trellised wall.

And then I found people
who needed more
than apartment, winter clothes.

They are with me all the time
twice twenty hours each day.
My people.
But there is so little I can do
that anyone can do
alone.

They are with me everywhere.
As I shampoo my Sita's tresses
I see Harjit
pinned to locker floor
by four of his schoolmates
while the fifth lopped off his hair

As my Mano
whacks mosquitoes off his bronzed back
I see the welts on Pritam's,
bruised by a drunken father.
Was drink the cause
or the result
of his joblessness?

Hasina, new bride from India
of one who lives common law
with Maria, mother of three,
two his.

Bihari, driven to suicide
in his basement bachelor suite
of six years.

Lata, caught between love
for her half-wit daughter
secreted away at an Ontario school,
And her husband's steel egotism
that wants no sign of his genetic flaw.

Azhar's mother homesick for windows,
encaged until the baby grows up
or Farida quits work.

My heart can hold them everyone
but not my head, which clamours
at the futility of it all.

And nearer home,
Usha's daughter, now blind,
wasting away like the moon
of an incurable and
many-tentacled disease.

**YOKIO** (*a woman from Japan*):

it is nature's way, they said
to throw out those unfit to see
the light of day.
and they dropped him in a white-lid jar
and carried him away.
threw him down the incinerator perhaps,
    flames sucking at those unformed lips
    that never will suckle here.
My son, heir to the heritage of the solar kings.

**SAPNA:** Dear Deedi, my sister,
In every letter over the last year, you have mentioned deaths in the family—of cousins, aunts, friends. And each time I have wept for the loss, but felt cut off, weeping so long after the event, here, ten thousand miles away. Everything is so distant, so far away. As though I am in a space bubble looking at a world orbiting in the distance that has forgotten me. But death, till now a distant stranger, knocked on our door last month, and we had to lay out one of our dearest friends. No matter how long we live here, our heart still yearns to touch the waters of the Ganga before it can go in peace to its eternal rest.

Gangajal, he said, I need Gangajal to wash him.
My heart contracted and exploded in fear.
I reached over to the alcove
Where we've enshrined our household gods,
And took down a cupsize copper pot
Sealed at a temple beside the holy river.
His hands were trembling as I placed it there,
And he had snowflakes in his hair.

We came together then, all of us,
two hundred and more;
and in the days that followed
there was more love in every home,
more compassion, less grievances
and gripes as each sought comfort
in wedded arms

and held on to those fragile bonds
which are never more hers to hold.

*Music interlude*

**CHORUS OF ALL ADULT SPEAKERS:**

We are New Canadians
Come from faraway places,
The Alps and the Andes,
Essequibo and the Ganges,
Our memories, our faces
Chiselled by ancient cultures
Whose courses had been half run
Long ere Cartier's had begun.

We are New Canadians
Come from many races
Black, white, olive, brown,
All alike, for all the many places
Hightech, midtech, notech
Are one.

We are New Canadians.
Same as the old, we grew
Ten moons in our mothers' womb,
Learnt to love, play and pray
On parents' knees.
Tasted youth's sadsweet greenness
And love's silver dreams.

Canada's fields are sown with gold,
Some said, and so it is.
It will not be easy, some said,
And it has not, as we all know,
Who have worked hard, or worse still,
Have no work at all, though willing
And waiting for the break
That would set us on our own.

What we were not told, never guessed,
Is written on our children's faces
Furrowed with tears because of our race,
Or colour, or tongue that stumbles
Over words so alien to the many places
From which we've come.

Will doors shut on them as on us?
Landlords', employers', universities'?
Have we come from the Niger and Luzon,
From the Antilles and Hong Kong,
To these vast empty spaces
Only to see our young ones faces
Slapped by unthinking scorn, unfeeling barbs,
From closed fists and closed hearts?

**GUULED** and **SAGAL** (*an old couple from Somalia*):
Under a sky bluer than any we've seen,
On snow whiter than ever we dreamed,
We stand beside the Golden Boy
Holding golden sheafs of corn
Against a dawn heralding the joy
Of years to come.

**SAPNA:** Dear Deedi, my sister,
We must build our temple here, here where the Assiniboine flows into the Red. And we shall bring Ganga, as Bhagirata did of old, to our land, our Assiniboine, and here shall be the groves where Uma shall dance with Parameswara.

*Dear Deedi, My Sister* won first prize in the *Caribe* play writing contest of 1989, and was published in *Caribe* (April, 1990)

# ROOTLESS BUT GREEN ARE THE BOULEVARD TREES

*CHARACTERS*

The Bhave family:
Sharad, the father
Savitri, the mother
Jayant, Jyoti, and Krish, their children
Veejala Moghe, Sharad's sister
Anant, Veejala's husband
Vithal and Priti, their children
Arun, Dilip, Rajen, and Sridhar, friends of Jayant and Vithal
Andre, Jyoti's boyfriend
Laura, Priti's friend

*Winnipeg, March-April, 1979. All scenes take place in the Bhave home in Fort Richmond.*

## ACT ONE

### Scene I

*Large built-up basement of a bungalow. The staircase divides the room into two unequal parts. The smaller section is brightly lit; the windows at either end of the room are half piled up with snow, and the light outside them shows it is afternoon. It is about three o'clock.*

*The sitting area is carpeted with a medium blue "hardtwist" carpet. The play area is tiled. There is a table tennis table half propped up, in the playback position. There are two heavy sponge bats on it and several balls. At the near corner is an open shelf with board games—Checkers, Yahtzee, Scrabble, Perquackey, neatly stacked. At the far end is a glass cabinet full of trophies. On the far wall is a dart board, and nine darts in a quill are on the table tennis table. Between the table and the dart board is an open suitcase and a large Adidas sports bag. At the edge of the table are a jogging suit and tennis and squash racquets.*

*Jayant is putting an album into its flap and walking toward his suitcase from the sitting area. He is nineteen years old, tall for an Indian, soft featured, wavy black hair falling just below his ears; the distinctive feature about him in this scene are his eyes, now smouldering black, angry.*

*Jyoti, twenty years old, in blue denims similar to Jayant's, is sitting between the suitcase and the dart board on a low ottoman. She is a beautiful girl, in hairstyle and dress typical of her age.*

*Krish, twelve, comes down the stairs.*

**KRISH:**Hi folks, howdee? Hope you aren't taking the whole collection, Jai.

**JAYANT:** Jeesus, no, you're welcome to all of it, kid. Got off early?

**KRISH**: How long will you be gone?

**JAYANT**: I've told you a dozen times if once, kid, if we can find our way to Europe, we'll be gone a year. If not—*(He shrugs.)*

**KRISH:** *(Moving from one foot to the other.)* I am going to miss you, Jeesus *(He unconsciously imitates his brother's mannerisms)*, especially on Wednesdays. The papers are so damn heavy. Can you give me a hand today?

**JAYANT:** Bug off, bozo, you and your paper route.

*Krish is not quite sure if Jai is being good humoured or angry. But when Jayant kicks the Adidas bag clear across the room after looking into it for something, Krish takes the cue and leaves, loudly whistling an Elton John tune to cover his disappointment.*

**JYOTI:** Krish and Dad, especially Dad, will miss you.

**JAYANT:** Let him. Time he knew he is never going to live his dreams through me. Jeesus, just because he was almost, but never, Number One, he's been after me all my life to drive that crummy ball ping ping back and forth.

**JYOTI:** No one can be so good at anything unless he enjoys doing it. Besides, I've seen your face when you are playing a match, so don't you try to pull that one on me.

**JAYANT:** Big deal. Provincial champ in a crappy basement game. *(He throws a dart at the board.)*

**JYOTI:** *(In a cool voice)* I am glad you are pitching out, and I sure hope it gets into that thick head of yours that we are different, and no matter what we do, we are never going to fit in here. Take to the road, get high, sleep around but still and all.

**JAYANT:** Fuck off, kid, you'll see.

**JYOTI**: All these expletives, all the in jargon, but you are never going to be one of the boys. Not that I see why anyone would want to fit into this mould.

**JAYANT:** Don't you come at me with all that crap about morals and Hindu values. I've had an earful from Dad nineteen fucking years. He and his pipe dreams about India. Why the hell didn't he stay there? An atomic energy scientist, he was right there from the beginning. . . . Trombay, planning, the whole bit. He'd have been a director by now. Instead he quits the place to be and rots here selling houses, Jeesus, a crappy real estate broker, just one step better than an encyclopedia salesman. . . .

**JYOTI:** *(Her face flushed with anger, is about to say something, but instead picks a high-bounce phosphorescent-coloured ball and whams it down on the floor. It bounces between floor and ceiling for the next few minutes as they speak.)* He's not a con man, for God's sake, people need houses *(more assertively)* and encyclopedias too.

**JAYANT:** Sure, sure, as much as they need a hole in the head. You know where I got my *Brittanica?* In the Miscellaneous Classifieds I saw this phone number with the price going down from three hundred to one hundred dollars over three weeks. And then I went there—a shitty little bedsitter—this young couple. God, nothing in that room cost more than twenty bucks, and here was the five-hundred-dollar *Brittanica* dumped on the sap by a smooth-talking salesman who had played up a sales pitch about self-education in applied electronics. Jeesus. And to think Dad has been one of those. *(He picks up a ping-pong ball and squeezes it in the palm of his left hand.)*

**JYOTI:** It couldn't have been easy for him to move out after he was thirty-five, and it is no bed of roses here, mowing the lawn and painting the house and a hundred menial chores which were done by servants in the luxury of family back home.

**JAYANT:** Some house that, a sprawling shambles handed down untouched from the time of the Peshwas, where you have to walk half a mile to get to the shithouse, Jeesus, we haven't lost anything on that count; even he couldn't think so. And I bet he wouldn't be so maudlin sentimental about that ancestral shack if he were back in Bombay.

**JYOTI:** And you wouldn't be mouthing vulgarities. Have you ever heard such uncouthness from Dad?—ever, ever?

**JAYANT:** He speaks like out of a book, a mighty bore of a Victorian book, too. Sententious half the time and sentimental the other half.

**JYOTI:** *(Sarcastically)* Maybe I spoke too soon, you are halfway to becoming one alright. Equating gentleness with effiminacy, affection with melodrama. *(Musingly, obviously quoting her father)* To live without tension and yet with dignity, to give our children good food, a liberal education, a healthy environment where, because the body doesn't have to scrounge for sustenance, the spirit can aspire to higher experiences than this sorry world allows.

**JAYANT:** And the irony is he isn't really sure whether he's given us all these out here. Jeesus, and you know what your trouble is, kid, you are on the moon with that sunshine boy, holding hands and singing moonshine. If you'd get laid a couple of times you'd come off all that preachy repetitions of Dad's slogans. Just get laid. *(He looks at her, and there is something in her eyes that draws him up sharply against the wall of recognition.)*

**JAYANT:** *(In a low voice)* You haven't, sis? You haven't. *(It is clear Jyoti has. Jayant is dazed, unwilling to accept it.)*

**JAYANT:** *(His voice far away)* Remember that mango tree in Chetan Das's yard back home? And all the raw green mangoes we stole? We never got caught once. And the lichees in Mussoorie that summer. God, they were succulent. And we never got caught then either.

**JYOTI:** *(Half sarcastically, half gently)* Good luck, bhau, and when you return to the fold, Dad will fix up an upper middle-class, fair-skinned, "homely" Brahmin, as all the matrimonial ads say when they mean "home loving." Virgin, of course.

*Jayant pulls the darts from the quill and zings them across the room in lightning sequence. All lodge in the inner circle, one dead centre. He picks up his jogging suit and blindly rushes up and out.*

## Scene II

*Same day, 4:30 P.M., in the kitchen.*

*The kitchen is a large rectangular room with a four-by-four-feet china cabinet with glass doors on both sides, which visually divides the dining area from the cooking area. On the top of the china cabinet are (eight-by-ten-inch) framed photographs of each of the children. The dining area is about fifteen feet wide by ten feet deep, while the cooking area is sixteen feet wide and six feet deep. A door, to the left, leads into the hallway to the bedrooms. Another door, to the right, leads to the living room. A door on the upper right leads to the landing and staircase. The dining area has a large window (eight by six feet) through which the sun is shining onto the dining table. In the yard outside are two tall poplars, leafless but shapely, their slender branches waving.*

*Savitri enters from the back door. She is thirty-nine, light brown, about five feet three inches tall. Her skin is marble smooth, her face comely. She takes off her gloves, places her handbag and a pile of scribblers on a chair, and takes off her boots while leaning against the wall. She takes the boots down the stairs and returns, taking off her coat. She is wearing a pantsuit—black pants, black and grey checked coat, and a silver grey blouse.*

*Krish enters from the hallway, hockey helmet in hand.*

**KRISH:** Hi, mom!

**SAVITRI:** *(Walking toward the hallway)* Rushing off already, beta? Is Jyoti home? Did you have anything to eat or drink? *(She takes an empty A & W mug, which Krish has obviously used, from the table to the sink. She exits, returning a moment later without her coat, jacket, and books.)*

**KRISH:** Had a large banana milkshake, mom, got rid of all the overripe bananas for you.

**SAVITRI:** *(Lifting the glass jar from the blender base and rinsing it off at the sink)* So I see, beta, so I see. *( She wipes the counter top.)*

**KRISH:** *(Ingratiatingly)* I'll put the kettle on for you. *(He turns on the stove with the kettle.)*

**SAVITRI:** *(Laughing)* You're a gold brick, beta. Is Jyoti home? *(She washes the teapot in hot water and takes out a teabag from it. She fills the kettle with fresh water.)*

**KRISH:** She was, but if she's still around, she's quiet as a mouse.

**SAVITRI:** *(Takes her books and bag and walks toward the hallway.)* Don't be late for dinner.

**KRISH:** No way. Hockey practice at seven. Can I have sixty-five cents mom, for skate sharpening? Just in case I forget later.

**SAVITRI:** *(Opening her bag.)* Anything else?

**KRISH:** Hot chocolate?

**SAVITRI:** *(Handing him a dollar)* Finished your paper route already?

**KRISH:** Yeah, we got off at three today.

*He sits on the steps and ties his boots. Savitri disappears into the hallway and returns, as the kettle whistles, wiping her face, which she has obviously washed. She puts the tea bag in the pot and pours the water. She switches off the stove. She goes out again and when she returns, she has kumkum on her forehead. Krish has meanwhile put on his coat, scarf, and gloves.*

**KRISH:** Bye, mom.

**SAVITRI:** Just check if Jyoti is downstairs, beta. *(She goes out into the hallway.)*

**KRISH:** *(After clomping down the stairs and up again.)* Nope, not here. Bye.

*Savitri comes in, tucking the pleats of her sari at her waist. She looks different now, very brown, very Indian, softly beautiful, and somewhat tired. She pours herself a cup of tea, takes the cup and saucer to the dining table and sits with her back to the window. She props her feet up on another chair. The sun shines on her back. She looks at the photograph of Jyoti on the china cabinet. The photograph shows a beautiful teenager whose eyes, looking just above the camera, are intriguingly sad and whose lips are turned up in a sullen smile.*

*Savitri's voice-over expresses her thoughts as she sips her tea and stares at the photograph.*

**SAVITRI:** *(Voice-over)*This still core of sadness that veils your eyes, this silence that pales your cheeks, when did you get it, my child, and why? Conceived in the flood tide of my love, reared in the springtime of my wealth, when did you get it, my child, and why? In your eyes I hoped to see the flash that brightens mine even now, in your voice I hoped to hear the song of the sky that comes even now to me though never so loud nor often. But you, in the flood tide of first love. . . . *(She sighs and sits for a moment, a tired look on her face. Then she gets up and energetically sets about getting dinner ready.)*

## Scene III

*Lights go up on the same scene.*

*Savitri is stirring something on the stove. Sharad comes in from the living room. He is forty-five, about five feet eight inches tall, and has a smiling face. He is dark complexioned and has a head of black and graying thick straight hair. He has a lean face and a long neck, which he tends to stick out so that his Adam's apple shows even clearer and he looks even taller than he is. Savitri makes him a cup of tea and hands it to him as he seats himself.*

**SAVITRI:** Some biscuits with your tea? Dinner'll be ready in a minute. Was that Jyoti?

**SHARAD:** No, that was the newsboy. What about Jyoti?

**SAVITRI:** Oh, nothing. I haven't seen her since yesterday morning, that's all.

**SHARAD:** You worry too much, Savi. She's alright. Growing to be a beauty, eh? Spit image of you at her age. When I look at the seeds of sadness in her eyes, she looks so much like you. I feel nostalgic and protective and silly. But then I remember how little you needed outside protection. Oh, you were a boarded-up door to those who didn't have a key.

**SAVITRI:** *(Placing biscuits on the table, she lightly touches Sharad's shoulder and they smile at each other)* You might like these.

**SHARAD:** How about a date tonight? Or are you going to be marking papers till two o'clock?

**SAVITRI:** Not unless you get hooked on the late night movie. *(Sharad pats her on her behind. There is an air of comradeship and being-in-love about them that has little to do with what they say.)*

**SAVITRI:** I wish Jyoti would come earlier nights.

**SHARAD:** Don't be a worrier, Savi. She's a good girl, and Andre is a decent boy. He behaves just like one of us. So respectful. And he looks like us too, with his black hair and eyes. Besides, you shouldn't continue to live in the prudish world of our youth. The youngsters here are doing well. They have their own code of morals and they are more idealistic than we give them credit for. This disco craze is perfectly harmless. *(In a tone of explanation as though he knows all about it and she knows nothing.)* A hundred youngsters swaying around; group activities are safety valves that this generation has discovered for itself. As long as they are in a group, they are alright. And thank God for our Winnipeg winters; nobody can wander into the bushes. Least of all *our* children. *(Savitri smiles sadly as* *she turns back to the counter. Jayant comes in.)*

**JAYANT:** *(Squarely placing his hands on his father's shoulder, he helps himself to a biscuit.)* Hi, Dad! How was your day? Did Mrs Christopher L. Jones make up her mind, the one who brings marbles to check the level of the floor in each room?

**SHARAD:** That's Mrs Pringle. Mrs Jones is the one who wants to be a half block away from her church. How's the car?

**JAYANT:** Guess the old girl is ready for the road but us guys aren't. Now that we are all packed, we are having second thoughts. Jim seems to have discovered he's much more involved with his girl than he'd thought. Dennis doesn't think he has enough bread to have the kind of ball he'd hoped to, out east. I'll have to wait for a weather change in them guys. I noticed your car's been in the garage all day, dad, anything wrong?

**SHARAD:** Nothing serious. I'd forgotten to plug in the block heater last night. Maybe I should check the battery.

**JAYANT:** Not on a three-year-old car, Dad. But if you wish, I could take it out and have it recharged overnight if necessary. *(He seats himself across from his father.)* Why didn't you wake me up? I could have helped booster from mom's car. You needn't have taken the bus.

**SHARAD:** *(Shaking his head)* I should take the bus more often and get used to it, son. It upsets me profoundly to find myself in a crowd. All those alien faces staring at or through you. It makes me wonder. Makes me ask myself, What am I doing here? Who are these faceless people among whom my life is oozing away? Each so self-contained, so complete, looking at me as though I shouldn't be there. It's a strange, eerie feeling, all those discreetly questioning eyes that make me ask endless questions.

**SAVITRI:** That is why I got myself a car. So I wouldn't have to ask myself questions that perhaps never can be answered. Not to our satisfaction.

**SHARAD:** How long can we live that way?

**JAYANT:** *(Good-humouredly)* To each his own hang-up. When I take a bus downtown, I love it. The Pembina strip is no big deal, an esthetic black hole in fact, but there's something that gets to one's guts even in this barren winter landscape, and suddenly from among the eyesore of billboards and bald trees you see man's indomitable spirit roaring to go up the ski slopes, even if with only a Stanfield brief to hold him up and Cougar boots that centrally heat his soul. Every time the bus goes over the midtown bridge I get a mighty kick thinking of the Indian canoes and the Bay company boats to whom the Red and Assiniboine were once vital lifelines.

**SHARAD:** *(Who has heartily laughed at Jayant's descriptions)* You've got something there, Jai, the fascination that rivers and mountains hold. That is why our people raised temples on every hillock and riverbank. Our people. . . .

**JAYANT:** *(Still good humoured but with an edge of impatience)* Our people, our old country, Dad, there's no "our people" and no "old country" for anyone in the world any more, least of all for us. This is our land and here we shall stay.

**SHARAD:** Roots, son, roots. Can we really grow roots here?

**JAYANT:** Sure, Dad, just look outside. The monstrous new apartment block out there—they have twenty-foot trees around the patio and there are five-footers inside the quadrangle, all set up overnight and flourishing like crazy. If anything, the pollution in the air seems to have acted like pep pills.

**SHARAD:** That would be a most reassuring analogy, Jai, if our poplar hadn't died. The centre branch didn't bloom last summer, if you remember, and you know what Dave next door said? They are Ontario poplars and not native to Manitoba, and so it is to be expected that they'd dry up one winter, just like that, he said. Looking at them now, who'd think one of them was dead?—that the core is dried up, that the sap isn't flowing up those beautiful branches that form so perfectly shaped a cone? One would think they'd been trimmed every year. If it doesn't bloom this spring, well, we'll have to cut it down. And if an Ontario poplar can't grow and survive in Manitoba soil, what chance do we have?

### Scene IV

*Same scene as before; the table is set for six but there are only five—Sharad, Savitri, Krish, Jayant, and Priti. Priti—or Pixie, as she is called—is nine years old and resembles Sharad in complexion, hair and eyes. Savitri, sitting at the foot of the table, near the counter, changes dishes, refills, puts them away as they are emptied, generally taking care of the meal and especially serving the younger two. Halfway through the meal, she puts away Jyoti's plate.*

**PRITI:** I have a yukky spoon. I need another one.
**SHARAD:** A Panchali spoon, eh?
**SAVITRI:** The dishwasher is acting up again, I think.
**JAYANT:** Let's call it Panchali. I too need another fork.
**PRITI:** Tell us the story, uncle, tell us.
**KRISH:** *(In mock despair)* Oh, no, not a bedtime tale!
**PRITI:** Shut up, Krish, close your earflaps.
**SHARAD:** Haven't you heard it often enough?
**PRITI:** I like uncle's stories.
**SHARAD:** One day, when the Pandavas and Panchali were in exile in the forest, Krishna visited them. They had just finished their meal and Panchali had already washed the pots and pans and so. . . .
**PRITI:** There was nothing left at all for Krishna.
**SHARAD:** That's right, and he said, "I'm hungry, sister, aren't you going to serve me dinner?" And Panchali thought, "Ohhh! What shall I do?"
**KRISH:** She didn't even know how to cook.
**PRITI:** She was a princess, fathead, princesses aren't supposed to cook.
**SAVITRI:** Do you know from where they got their meal, Krish?
**KRISH:** Oh, mom! I know the story.
**PRITI:** Go on, uncle, go on.
**SHARAD:** Well, Krishna said he wanted to see the pot in which Panchali had made the rice.
**PRITI:** Spinach!
**KRISH:** Oh, yuk!

**SHARAD:** Why spinach?

**PRITI:** Don't you remember we changed it last time from rice to spinach?

**KRISH:** Doesn't make sense. Cooked rice dries up and sticks to a pot more than spinach.

**PRITI:** Shut up.

**KRISH:** You shut up yourself.

**SAVITRI:** Children, children! Is someone forgetting something?

**PRITI:** I'm sorry.

**JAYANT:** Krish?

**KRISH:** *(With an effort)* Okay, okay, I'm sorry.

**PRITI:** Ouch.

**JAYANT:** *(To Krish in a low voice)* Quit it, kiddo. *(To Priti)* Did he kick you?

**PRITI:** *(Unwilling to reply)* Let's forget it.

**JAYANT:** *(Scooping out some ice cream to refill Priti's fruit bowl)* That' s a sport, Pixie, you haven't said anything about school.

**PRITI:** We have a wall put in our room. The room is so small it's gross.

**JAYANT:** Be glad you have a wall. The first school I went to had no walls, only a thatched roof.

**PRITI:** Really?

**JAYANT:** Yes, really. Granddad started it for the kids on the estate. I was too young to go to regular school and so I'd go there and sit with the kids until lunchtime. Remember, Dad, how the roof flew away that second year? And all the baby mangoes fell off the trees?

**PRITI:** Were you in class?

**JAYANT:** Nah. I was at St Michael's already. But we didn't have school that day. And panditji quoted some Kabir dohe as we ran toward the cowsheds. He was forever singing Kabir songs.

**KRISH:** Tell us, Jai, tell us how you used to call him "two-eyes" because he was cockeyed.

**PRITI:** *(Aggrieved.)* What's that? You've never told me. . . .

**JAYANT:** We knew his eyes were different from ours but I guess we were stupid or something, eh?

**PRITI:** Oh, because we all have two eyes, right? So what else about him?

**KRISH:** Jai tells me neat stories. He's a real brother.

**PRITI:** *(On whom the barb has hit home)* Vithal doesn't have time, that's why.

**KRISH:** Betcha don't know about how the toilet in granddad's house didn't have no roof one time for a long time.

**PRITI:** Really?

**JAYANT:** And the bakul flowers would fall on us as we did our jobs, oops, sorry, not at the table. *(He makes an exaggerated gesture of apology)* So, how are your cartwheels, Pixie?

**PRITI:** Oh, yeah, I forgot to tell you. Your way really works. Thanks, Jai.

**JAYANT:** Any time, Pix. Here, have half a banana.

**PRITI:** Do I have to?

**JAYANT:** A banana a day keeps all problems away. Remember, dad, my banana cluster in granddad's house .

**KRISH:** *(Aside)* Whew, why this "remember" binge today?

**SHARAD:** Pixie, this was a tree we planted on Jai's first birthday and by the time we left, it was a grove .

**PRITI:** Did you plant one every birthday?

**SHARAD:** No, not quite, but banana trees have a way of multiplying themselves; there's a saying: "a banana tree always leaves a young tree in its shade."

**KRISH:** *(In a sing-song voice)* And every part of the banana tree is useful—its fruit, its leaves as plates, its fibre as string, ta da ta da ta da. *(Jayant is about to reprove Krish but Savitri signals him to desist.)*

**JAYANT:** Kiddo, I'll have to take you there for you to understand these things . You haven't ever seen a banana tree .

**KRISH:** There's one in the greenhouse at the Assiniboine Park.

**PRITI:** Mom said she'd take me to the park last weekend. And the weekend before that. She never did.

**SAVITRI:** Your mom is a very busy person, Priti.

**PRITI:** Everyone is busy all the time. Busy, busy, busy.

**JAYANT:** Almost time for *The Littlest Hobo*. Finish your ice cream quickly, Pixie-Trix.

**PRITI:** Will you watch with me?

**KRISH:** Kid stuff.

**SAVITRI:** Your mom tells me you watch far too much TV.

**PRITI:** Yeah, but I don't enjoy it unless someone watches it with me.

**KRISH:** Jai, will you play Othello with me!

**JAYANT:** *(Patting him on the head)* You're getting too good for me kiddo. *(Krish is flattered for a moment but sees himself defeated at getting Jai for himself. His face falls. Jayant notices that but evades direct reversal.)*

**JAYANT:** But I'll tell you what. I'll take you on if it's Chinese Checkers.

**KRISH:** My way? Jumping over blank holes on each side allowed!

**JAYANT:** K.O. Your way.

**PRITI:** But aren't you gonna watch tv with me?

**JAYANT:** Don't you know me? Napoleon used to dictate four different letters or war plans or whatever to four different people at the same time. Can't you trust me to do two things at once? *(Jayant, Krish, and Priti leave for the living room.)*

**SAVITRI:** He has a way with children. They're going to miss him. Especially Priti. Poor child.

**SHARAD:** Fancy him remembering about that thatched roof!

**SAVITRI:** I've grown used to your nostalgia trips, but this is something new in Jai. But he's your son, after all. *(She smiles)*

**SHARAD:** My son. God bless him.

## Scene V

*Basement. Same scene as I, except that the ping-pong table has been unfolded to the play position. Jayant's bags, etc. are now under the table. Jayant is kneeling on the floor, transferring the last of the contents from a suitcase to the floor. As he speaks, he puts them one by one into a slightly larger suitcase. Vithal comes in. He is two years older than Jayant but looks more of a man. Feature for feature, he resembles his cousin but the resemblance is obscured by the difference in their personalities. Vithal is an angry young man, though his face transforms into that of a pleasant youngster when he smiles. He has a moustache, and the attractive hirsuteness of one whose beard grows fast. Jayant's face lights up on seeing Vithal. Though*

*Jayant is a couple of inches taller, it seems that whenever they look at each other Jayant is looking up and Vithal down.*

**VITHAL:** *(Holding a car compass)* I almost forgot to give you this. It is still functional, but I'd suggest you buy another more reliable one. Worth the few extra bucks, I can tell you. Those roads in the Laurentians could be one hell of a maze once you get off the highway. By the way, I did tell you about the quirks of the luggage rack, right?

**JAYANT:** Instead of all these directions and instructions, why don't you join us, Vith? Come along. *(He gets excited as he speaks.)* Come on Vith, I've been wanting to ask you all along. Wow, we'd have a ball. Please. We could leave the rest of the gang in Montreal; they want to hang out there for a while, a coupla weeks with Don, Don Blackwood, remember him? We can take off on that canoe trip you've always wanted. Montmorenci. . . . Come on, Vithal. This is the time. *(Vithal says nothing. He continues to bounce a ball low on the table, bringing the bat slowly down. The sound of the drawn-out crunch provides a background song.)* I've had some great times, Vith, but the greatest have been with you, when it was just us two. Jeez, the things you've taught me! I was one raw hunk of a kid in '72. Didn't know even how to tie a slipknot. But the things I knew by the time we returned! And then our summer in India. *(He whistles)*I thought we were packed off there for granddad's sixtieth birthday just to please the folks back home, and I hated leaving Winnipeg. But Jeez, that was the best time I've ever had. We were a great team, remember the time in Delhi we lost our way near Sikander Tomb and. . . . Oh, Vithal, please do come. Say the word and I'll drop out of the gang. Who needs them anyhow? But we have to get out of this asshole. We are just killing ourselves here. Parents are such a pain in the ass, let's go. I can't stand them.

**VITHAL:** *(With startling vehemence)* Quit talkin', fella, running away, that's all everyone thinks of, run away, tuck your tail between your legs and scram the moment some problem comes up. But you, you want someone to hang on to even when running away. You've done nothing but hang on to apron strings all your life. And all the time ranting all that bullshit about growing up and being on your own. You are just one hell of a mixed-up bounder. Deep inside, all you want is to suck your thumb and dream of granddad's estate. You're pissed off, Jayant; you and your hangups; resenting your dad because he is in some humdrum business and not a superscientist; and yet you are emotionally tied to his coattail; one harsh word from him and you are ready to snivel like a sissy schoolgirl.

Oh, man, isn't it time you were to someone what he's been to you? What I've been to you? What every goddam person around you has been to you? Instead of being an obnoxious leech with a thumbsucking ego?

All you can think of is running away. Run away, like a coward. God, I'm sick of you, sick of the whole lot of runners away.

*Vithal's onslaught has annihilated Jayant. He sits there, looking up with pained bafflement, a dog that has been suddenly kicked by his master. He gets up slowly from his crouched stance on the floor, slowly collects ping-pong balls from the floor and sofas, and mechanically drops each with trembling fingers into a Halex carton. The chore composes him somewhat, but he still has a dazed expression. Vithal, meanwhile, is leaning his elbow against the near wall, bat in hand, holding his head.*

**VITHAL:** *(In a subdued way)* I am sorry, Jay, taking it out on you like that. I . . . I have problems. I'm sorry.

**JAYANT:** *(Eagerly accepting the apology)* We are all made that way, I guess, a family of volcanoes, except for Jyoti. I wish . . . do you know that Jyo. . . . Let's play. *(Takes up a bat.)*

**VITHAL:** *(Without moving)* Mom is leaving us.

**JAYANT:** *(Shocked)* No! She can't do that. *(Whispers)* That's all over long ago. . . . She can't do that! *(His voice breaking)* What are we going to do? Jeesus, what we gonna do?

**VITHAL:** *(Comes to the table and takes out a ball from the carton)* I think I've found a way to return that double spin of yours. Here. Rally.

## Scene VI

*The next day, lunch hour.*

*Savitri comes down the basement steps, calling "Jyoti!" The hi-fi is on full volume. The sitting area lights up. Jyoti is on the couch, her feet on an ottoman. There are text books all around. She reaches out and turns down the volume on the hi-fi. Savitri comes in. She is in her school outfit, with a cardigan instead of a jacket. By habit, as she talks she puts things back in place—magazines off the television top into the magazine rack, socks off the floor, etc.*

**SAVITRI:** *(Without looking at Jyoti after the first glance.)* I don't want you to use your father's car in the evening from now on. Any time you need a car, take mine, and if I have to go out again after work, I shall take dad's car. Is that clear?

**JYOTI:** What's the big deal? There isn't a scratch on the Chrysler, not from me. So what's the to-do?

**SAVITRI:** Because.

**JYOTI:** We outgrew that reason ten years ago, mother.

**SAVITRI:** *(With sudden vehemence)* Yes, we are supposed to treat you as rational adults even when you behave like beasts. *(She takes out an open condom pack from her cardigan pocket and flings it against the back of the recliner)* I don't know whether you want to prove something to me or whether you meant to flaunt this to your father or what, but I don't want this to happen in dad's car, ever.

**JYOTI:** Big deal, mom, it was just an accident that it dropped out. I didn't even know. And who needs a car for that, anyway. As for dad, what makes you think he'll flip his lid any more than you? You help him on with his blinkers night and day, you trot him out and into his ivory tower all the time, but surely no one could have lived here ten years without. . . .

**SAVITRI:** How long has this been going on?

**JYOTI** :*(Mockingly)* I don't think you'd like the answer to that.

**SAVITRI:** *(Taken aback, she pulls herself together with an effort.)* I'll take you to Doctor MacRae and put you on the pill. *(She shrugs. Maybe I'm out of date there too, maybe a mother is not* *needed anymore even for that. (With firmness)* But you will go to him, Jyoti. *(Then she adds after a pause)* If you haven't already, of course.

**JYOTI:** *(Picks up the pack and sticks it into her handbag.)* Ramses! Damn romantic name for a goddam rubber.

**SAVITRI:** *(Startled by the bitterness in the girl's voice, she moves forward.)* Jyoti. . . . *(Jyoti turns away.)*

**SAVITRI:** *(Mockingly)* If that's how blase you are about it, I pity you, Jyoti, I pity you.

**JYOTI:** *(Collecting several of her books, speaks with studied casualness.)* I'd better run before you get behind your lectern. *(She leaves)*

**SAVITRI:** *(Her hands on the back of the recliner, she stands still while the voice-over comes on.)* Ramses. When you said that, my darling, I wanted to hold you to myself, lick away your tears, soothe smooth away your fears, take you back into myself and wrap you and keep you. Instead I spoke to you as to a woman, someone not myself, a woman who wanted to hurt and claw.

## ACT TWO

### Scene I

*Saturday morning, about 11:00 A.M.*

*Jyoti is having breakfast in the kitchen. She is in blue jeans and a loose, open-collared shirt. The doorbell rings. Jyoti goes toward the living room. Sound of door opening and Jyoti effusively greeting someone. Sridhar and Jyoti enter kitchen. In looks and speech, Sridhar is different from the other young men. The lilt in his accent and his vocabulary show he has been educated in India's public schools. He is darker than the others and has a hairline that recedes at the left. He is not good-looking but has an intellectual and sensitive face that makes him stand out in any company.*

**SRIDHAR:** Why the welcome mat? Something wrong? Did Krish beat you at Othello? Andre not turn up? Mom refuse you the car? Prof. make mincemeat of your term paper?

**JYOTI:** *(Laughing)* A little of everything. But mainly it is Saturday morning. That's why. Do I look that beaten up? How did you know I was feeling driven up the wall?

**SRIDHAR:** Been sitting three years on your doorstep, remember? Where's everyone?

**JYOTI**: Mom and dad have gone shopping

**SRIDHAR:** Dad shopping?

**JYOTI:** A haircut maybe, while mom shops. I dunno. Krish must be somewhere in the bay. And Jayant's under the car as usual, I suppose, at Jim's.

**SRIDHAR:** Some host. Invites me for lunch and disappears.

**JYOTI:** For lunch? Are you sure?

**SRIDHAR:** Of course I am sure. Not just me. The whole gang, he said, since this might be his last weekend.

**JYOTI:** Lunch, eh? *(Gets up and starts clearing the table.)* I'd better get something started. Mom's expecting you all for dinner. *(Opens oven)* Yes, there's matter paneer all made. But nothing else. Might as well put the boiler on for a quick pilav. *(Takes out rice boiler, fills it with water and measures out rice as they talk.)*

**SRIDHAR:** Have they decided just when they are hitting the road?

**JYOTI:** Haven't a clue. As soon as they can get the jalopy in shape, I guess. It is spring everywhere else. *(She turns toward Sridhar)* Have you taken a look at it, Shri? Is it really safe? It didn't look anything like a car when they brought it in first.

**SRIDHAR:**They know what they are doing. Jim has fixed up a neat ramp at his own place. They are pros.

**JYOTI:** But you are in mechanical engineering, and you've been right into car building. You'd know better.

**SRIDHAR:** No one's asked me and I am not a guy that butts in.

**JYOTI:** Why so formal?

**SRIDHAR:** Mine's only book knowledge. Jim and Dennis have worked in garages summers since they were aye high.

**JYOTI**: *(With a quick glance at him)* Is that what they say or how you feel?

**SRIDHAR:** *(With a sheepish smile)* A little of both, I guess. Just one of those hangups we grad students have when we come up against real-life mechanics.

**JYOTI:** Shri, I'd feel happier if you would check the car. They don't even have the right tools, just some primitive throwaways. Please.

**SRIDHAR:** *(Bowing)* Anything you say, ma'am. Any time, ma'am. *(They laugh.)*

**JYOTI:** You're a sport. I feel so comfy with you. *(She takes a cauliflower out of the refrigerator and cuts it as they talk.)*

**SRIDHAR:** I should feel flattered. If I didn't know something was up. What is it? Here's a shoulder to cry on.

**JYOTI:** I'll take a raincheck on that, because things aren't all that bad yet. Everyone's a bit nervy with Jayant all set to go, that's all. It is nice to have someone to talk to, someone to growl at, someone to laugh with, someone who knows all about the family. As a matter of fact, everything is dandy! It is great to be alive and in love.

**SRIDHAR:** With Andre. And me rooted to your doorstep three years. *(He throws up his hands in mock despair.)*

**JYOTI:** Oh, be serious.

**SRIDHAR:** Okay, okay. *(He literally wipes a grin off his face.)* What's your problem?

**JYOTI:** It is not a problem. Everything is so extreme—so ecstatic and so depressing, so high and so low. And I am so inarticulate. He used to think I was cold blooded because I never let on.

**SRIDHAR:** *(Stiffens momentarily and then shrugs exaggeratedly)* Never let on about clammy hands and shortwindedness, tingle and all, right? But you can talk to me about it, right? Third-person syndrome, right? *(Jyoti does not say anything but the colour rises on her cheeks.)* And your slide projector inside keeps shooting a million angles of the same face, right?

**JYOTI:** *(Changing the subject)* Will you be going to Detroit with that electric car for the show?

**SRIDHAR:** Does he feel that way? Does he really, really feel that way? That's the nagging question, right?

**JYOTI:** *(Provoked)* Of course he does. Every fibre in your being can't quiver unless the vibes are mutual.

**SRIDHAR:** *(Passionately)* Can't it, God, can't it? *(Recovering his usual flamboyance)* Every nerve, every hair erect, and not just hair, I can tell you.

**JYOTI:** *(With biting coolness)* That sounds like a wisecrack you've been rehearsing "to tell the boys."

**SRIDHAR:** *(Stung to the quick, he flares up)* Damn you, I must be mad to come here. God, how I wish I could hate and have done with you. Time was all of Winnipeg was brighter because of you, every day a gateway to Eden and I would go to sleep touching the tips of your fingers. But now I can't get to sleep until I have exhausted myself ripping you up, until I rape and rip you apart night after night. Damn you and damn that s.o.b. Adonis of yours. *(He walks out of the room. Sound of front doors slamming shut. Jyoti continues to cut the cauliflower, her face hidden by her hair.)*

## Scene II

*Lights up again on the same scene but with Jyoti placing a lid on a skillet on the stove. Sound of back door being opened. Sound of boots being scraped, and of voices. Jayant enters first, and as he speaks, others enter one by one—Arun, Vithal, Rajen, and Dilip.*

**JAYANT:** Hi mom! Mom? Oh, hi, Jyoti, something smells good. What a sport. Thanks, Jyo, I meant to phone mom we were coming for lunch, not dinner, but before I knew it, wham, it was lunch time. Was that Shri whipping out of the bay at a hundred miles an hour? He told you about lunch, I suppose. Did you send him out to buy something?

Come on you guys. Looks like we're going to get lunch sooner than I thought, but we'd better have something anyway. How about mango sundae?

*He takes out a can of mango pulp and fixes up the blender with milk and vanilla ice cream. The others, meanwhile, have greeted Jyoti, all except Dilip. Jayant draws up a chair for Dilip and introduces him.*

Sorry for not doing the honours properly—Jyoti this is Dilip; he's just come from IIT Delhi this term. And this is my sis. Sit down fellows. *(He goes back to his milkshake making.)*

**VITHAL:** Let me help with something. What's cooking?

**JYOTI:** *(Pleased to see him)* That's anybody's guess. Mom's made enough mattar paneer to feed an army and pilav will be ready as soon as the vegetables are done. Any suggestions?

**VITHAL:** How about puris? I haven't had a good Indian meal in ages. Here, I'll get the dough ready. Arun, it is time you washed your eyes; slice some onions for raita.

*He is obviously familiar with the kitchen, and in a trice has mixing bowl, flour, etc. on the table. Sound of back door opening. Sridhar enters.*

**JAYANT:** Come on in, Shri. the way you vroomed away I thought you were out to kill.

**SRIDHAR:** *(His usual self now)* Me kill? Gentle as a baa lamb. If anything, I am just a wet doormat for people to walk over. *(He sits down. Jyoti and he do not look at each other directly at any time. He takes out a scratch pad and doodles and draws through the scene.)*

**VITHAL:** Arun, what were you moaning about this evening?

**ARUN:** *(Taking onion and knife)* Yeah, I can't make it. I have to be at the International Students' at eight.

**JAYANT:** That crappy joint? How can you stand it?

**ARUN:** I am stuck with it for the year. Thank God it is almost over.

**JAYANT:** You kidding? You know the type. A cross between do-gooders and husband hunters.

**ARUN**: Come on, be fair.

**JAYANT:** Okay, I'll be fair. I haven't met anyone there with a semblance of good looks or intelligence but many with hearts of gold.

**RAJEN:** Met the other kind anywhere?

**JAYANT:** You have a point, man, they don't come in that brand any more.

**RAJEN:** They must be somewhere. Drat it. When I first came, everyone knew everyone else, but now there are such droves of them you don't get to know anyone. We can't seem to find any smart girls. Present company excepted, of course.

**JYOTI:** Thanks.

**RAJEN:** Tell me, Jyoti, what's the matter with girls, Indian girls, I mean. One tries to say a friendly hello and they freeze up like we were making a pass.

**ARUN** :What gets my goat is the way they all honey munch with others. It shames the pants off us to see our girls smiling sweety sweet with everyone but us. They need to get their noses punched.

**RAJEN:** Sure, go ahead, if you can reach above their belly buttons, that is. Or do you mean to punch the girls' noses!

**ARUN**: Three girls, yessiree three got hitched up this year. And I could name a dozen who are going steady or going out anyway.

**JYOTI:** There are three hundred who didn't.

**ARUN:** Them. They are so conservative they'd wear purdah if their dads told them to.

**DILIP:** *(In an aside to Sridhar)* The other day I was at the Shahs' and there were quite a few young people. It reminded me of back home.

**ARUN** : Three girls! Not one, not two, girls are such dum dums.

**RAJEN:** Present company excepted, of course .

**VITHAL:** No need to except it, dammit. Tell us Jyoti, man to man, why this rash of dating whites? And don't come up with the usual nonsense about love at first sight.

**RAJEN:** And keep off the double standards bit as well. We guys have to mumbo jumbo white girls only because our own girls are such touch-me-nots.

**JYOTI:** What can I say? You've forbidden both logical answers there are.

**VITHAL:** Logic, my ass. Love at first sight is baloney. One falls in love for the qualities one sees.

**JYOTI:** A dozen people around may have those qualities, but you happen to fall for a particular one. It just happens.

**SRIDHAR:** Vibes, man, vibes. *(He gesticulates with his fingers.)* Supersensory antennae zoom like a jack-in-the-box the moment Prince Charming appears.

**RAJEN:** Or Princess Charming. Let's not be sexist.

**ARUN:** But aren't we off the track? Who's talking about love and marriage! Just sitting together over a pizza, a movie maybe .

**RAJEN:** Oh, that? No squeezing hands and maybe hmm. *(Several laugh.)*

**JAYANT:** *(In a cool voice but with undertone of vehemence)* That's the problem, you guys are so naive, the most you can think of is squeezing hands. Maybe if you offered to screw them you'd have them at your feet.

**ARUN:** Easy, easy, there's a limit to jokes in mixed company.

**VITHAL:** Jyoti's okay. She's one of us. You still haven't answered, though.

**JYOTI:** Oh, I didn't think you wanted an answer. You are all like the six blind men and the elephant, each talking about a different thing altogether. And liking the sound of your own voice, no matter what the other guys say. But that is alright, because there are as many types of dating as you can think of and girls for every type, if you 'd just stop talking and do something. Ask Dilip about the three hundred girls you've rejected out of hand now. You guys notice only the few who do something a bit off the beaten path.

**RAJEN:** *(Aside)* A Freudian slip that?

**JYOTI:** As for dating local style, we have to change with time. Haven't we been in the closet long enough? I don't mean just girls. All of us.

**JAYANT:** *(Half mockingly)* Say, that's profound, ain't it? We have to change. Sounds so good when you say it, and yet you know what? Just the other day someone said just the opposite and it sounded even better. "Take to the road, get stoned, sleep around but you'll never become one of them. Why anyone would want to become one of them beats me," those were the words.

**DILIP:** *(Somewhat hesitantly, feeling a newcomer in a closed group and yet eager to speak)* But, it seems to me, you should make every effort to merge since you are here to stay. I mean, this is your country, the only land you know and will know. You have to try to assimilate, don't you think? The whites would appreciate that effort.

**VITHAL:** Assimilate, my ass. They don't want us to assimilate. They want us out. We'll be squashed like bugs soon. All these years we thought the isolation was coming from us, but now that we are trying to merge we know exactly what they feel. They've never wanted us and now we are a threat. Serves us right for wanting to try to be one of them. We have to stay separate from them and stay together within and we've got to show them that we have as much right to be here as the pissed-off whites who've bullied their way into this country these last three hundred years. We've got to stay apart, stay together. That's the only way.

**DILIP:** *(Impressed but still puzzled)* But what's the point of living in ghettoes?

**RAJEN:** Good word, yaar. But that's called multiculturalism out here. Each group stays together and once a year there's a three-ring circus, a zoo called Folkorama where everyone visits everyone else's cage. Hula, Calypso, bagpipes and all. Just wait for the mela. I'll take you around. Except that everyone gets drunk after about ten every night.

**VITHAL:** *(Continuing as though Rajen hadn't spoken)* Ghettoes is right. But we need ghettoes. Look at the Jews. They've been ghettoed for centuries and they've chosen to ghetto themselves even if they didn't have to. Only in ghettoes can unity thrive. They toughened themselves, did everything five times better than the others and now they don't get pushed around any more. They are top of the world.

**RAJEN:** Now that they are the tops, now that they are accepted and all that, do you see the writing on the wall? They are disintegrating, just melting into the sea of society. They are dying, in short. What an anti-climax. Tst. Tst. No more Einsteins, or even Philip Roths. They'll be finished. Schlemiel, schlimazel, shlep, kvetch, all gone; knish, blintz, borscht, all gone. Oi vey!

**VITHAL:** Don't fool around, man. We've got to stand tall. And by

God we shall. We shall build our temple at the confluence of the Red and Assiniboine and then we shall say Okay, we are ready to assimilate. Not here not now. Now it'll be bootlicking, applepolishing.

**ARUN:** Come on, Vith old man. I thought you'd have grown out of the Naxalite phase by now.

**VITHAL:** Go ahead, be patronizing. But if your house gets stones and eggs smashed on the window, you'll get action faster from them than from any goddam cop. That's the writing on the wall, that we can't expect nothing from these pissed-off bastards. Living like goddam ostriches, that's what we are.

**ARUN:** How are your Desh Hall friends? Haven't seen them around campus for quite a while.

**VITHAL:** *(Suddenly quiet)* I don't go there any more. *(Everyone falls silent, infected by Vithal's sudden depression. Realizing that, Vithal rallies.)*

**VITHAL:** I have personal problems, boys. I am too busy making it to hell on my own to bother about missionary zealots.

**ARUN:**Anything we can do to help?

**RAJEN:** We'll sock it to her. Gently but firmly. Just tell us who. With a Don Juan like you, we wouldn't want to bonk the wrong one.

**VITHAL:** I'll do it myself. Thanks anyway. More milkshake there?

**JAYANT:** *(Passing the milkshake)* Vithal, you sound good, man, but your arguments are a washout. Why should we fall on the neck of bastards who'd be way out of our orbit in India? One makes one's friends for their qualities, as you yourself said, not for their skin colour. Face it, man, we don't have anything in common with the other half of the Indians here. Why the hell do we have to rub shoulders with them simply because we happen to come from the same political entity? That's all India is, a political entity that came together as a nation after a zillion years because the British made it so.

**VITHAL:** British, my ass.

**JAYANT:** Cool it, man, I know my history as well as you. Asoka, Akbar, Aurangzeb—all ruled all of India but they didn't have a nation, not by a long shot.

**RAJEN:** Don't forget Sivaji, Jai Bhavani, Har Har Mahadev ki Jai.

**JAYANT:** *(Lightly giving him an uppercut on his right jaw)* No one makes fun of Sivaji under this roof. But no one.

**RAJEN:** *(Gamely)* How about Ram Rajya?

**DILIP:** *(Leaning forward excitedly)* You can't use that flippant tone for Ram Rajya. It has held us together from within. Rama, Krishna, Govinda—that's the essential truth, and because of that we've been a nation for five thousand years!

**JAYANT:** Right ho, sir, but let's come to *us*. Why in sacred hell, give me one solid reason in hell, why we should paw around with illiterates who troop into airports carrying kerosene tins and bedding rolls. I've seen them, Jeesus, mucking up all of Heathrow with stinking masalas and turbans. And *(He turns to Vithal)* I have news for you and your favourite story about the *Komagata Maru.* I'll come to that in a sec. *(He continues to speak and gesticulate but his voice is not heard while Rajen is heard in an aside to Dilip.)*

**RAJEN:** *(Aside to Dilip)* This was a ship chartered by a Sardarji back in 1914 to circumvent the immigration regulation that said colonials immigrating into Canada had to come straight from a British colony direct into Canada. It was Canadian Immigration's sneaky way of preventing brown immigrants, since there was no direct service between Canada and the Far East. This ship—*Komagata Maru*—was quarantined and starved off Vancouver for a month and then the passengers were shunted back to India, a shameful, ignominous episode for everyone concerned.

**JAYANT:** That guy who chartered it—Gurdip Singh—was a cheapskate two-bit crook who was leading four hundred suckers who thought they could get rich quick. Skidrow bums led by a scoundrel. I read a book about it.

**RAJEN:** Really? Where'd you get it, yaar?

**VITHAL:** I know the book. Written by a white, what else could you expect?

**RAJEN:** Sure, sure. Whites would whitewash the white barbarism, and a brown writer would tan the whites. What the saga needs is an impartial outsider, a Chinese. But you never can tell. Yellow is nearer to white than brown. Tst, tst.

**JAYANT:** Quit kidding, Jeesus, these scum bums.

**ARUN:** Easy, easy, forget your lord-of-the-manor past, Jay, this is a classless society.

**VITHAL:** Shows how little you know about this society. But hang classlessness, and what have you. It's a plain question of survival. If we don't stand together, we don't have a chance.

**JAYANT:** Count me out. They've brought nothing but a bad name on us. Getting convicted for rape and murder.

**ARUN:** Easy, easy, when there are a hundred thousand people, there's bound to be a couple crooks and maniacs among them.

**VITHAL:** I agree, you guys, but do you read the story between the lines, the editorial slant of how quick they are to identify the colour and country of the few who get into trouble? Exploiters and sensationalists.

**JAYANT:** Why don't you talk about the exploiting slave drivers out west? That show last Saturday just about killed me.

**VITHAL:** What show?

**RAJEN:** It was a documentary on farmhelpers in B.C.

**JAYANT:** We were at Larry's watching the game. I had the remote control, and commercial time I switched channels, and there it was—poor illiterate Panjabis bundled off into unheated shacks. And who was their employer? A son of a gun Panjabi. I was so paralyzed with shame I couldn't press the damned button to change channels. Jim was decent enough to pass it off with a "C'mon you guys, get back to the game."

**VITHAL:** You have a decent lot of friends. I'll hand that to you and to them. Real decent guys, and I'd be proud of you if your head wasn't screwed the wrong way.

**RAJEN:** Hey, Sri, you haven't said a word. Open up, yaar, let's have your words of wisdom.

**SRIDHAR:** *(Who has been doodling intricate border designs on his pad)* I think I know what Vithal's getting at. Jay gets so het up because he identifies himself emotionally with every brown face he sees. Vithal, on the other hand, is far more detached despite his fanaticism. He's calling for political identification, or coalition rather.

**RAJEN:** Hear hear, Mr Speaker.

**SRIDHAR:** Okay, I know I sound like a pretentious sociologist, but I mean, hell, why does it have to be "them" and "us" all the time, why not just you and me, an individualistic approach; the best bet is to let time take its course, and come a couple of generations everything would be more even all around, within the community and outside; we'd have a lot more brown-white kids and the problems. . . .

**RAJEN:** As Mrs Rabbit said to Mr Rabbit when they were chased by the hunting dogs, hang on a while longer and we'll outnumber. . . .

**ARUN** :You know what you sound like, Sri? *(He lifts his hand in a Nazi salute)* Heil Hitler! Heil Idi Amin! Forced marriages for a new improved race.

**RAJEN:** And Heil Margaret Thatcher, though she doesn't know it is the same thing.

**VITHAL:** People get what they deserve. And our history shows just what we deserve. Tyrants and traitors. Bin Tughlak, Sirajuddin Dowla, Jalianwala Bagh.

**ARUN**: And our liege lady who is staging a comeback.

**RAJEN:** Tyrants, traitors, and? You need another category for Sterling Lyon and Joe Clark. *(Everyone laughs except Vithal.)*

**VITHAL:** *(Suddenly more violently explosive than ever before)* Goddamned ostriches and cowards. Utterly selfish, that's what we are. Damn, double damn. *(He punches the dough.)*

*Sound of the back door opening. Savitri comes in, grocery bags in both arms. The boys take the bags from her. Rajen slips into his boots and goes out. Arun is about to follow but Savitri stops him.*

**SAVITRI:** Don't go. There are only two more bags. *(She goes down to the landing and comes back without her boots and with coat in hand.)* Hullo, boys. I am glad to see you. I do hope you won't forget us altogether once Jayant leaves. How is your mother's arm, Arun? Thank you, Rajen. *(Rajen says something.)* Yes, I know, he told me he'd be back in half an hour. Here, let me take over. Down you go, boys, and come up again in half an hour. Don't start any long-drawn game or debate. Lunch will be ready soon.

**RAJEN:** Take your time, Mrs Bhave, we're stuffed for the nonce. With Jay's milkshake and Vithal's speeches. *(All the boys, ex-*

*cept Vithal, go down. Vithal continues to knead the dough.)*

**SAVITRI:** Jyoti, thanks for starting the lunch. I thought they were coming for dinner!

**JYOTI:** You know Jayant, mom.

**SAVITRI:** It's wonderful to have a houseful of voices. I do hope they continue to drop in.

## Scene III

*Same scene as before.*

**SAVITRI:** *(Goes to Vithal and touches his arm.)* How are you, beta? You haven't been here since a long time. You are coming to the university everyday, aren't you? *(She waits expectantly but Vithal only smiles at the dough.)* You haven't dropped any courses, have you?

**VITHAL:** *(Looks up and smiles pleasantly)* No, but only because I'd forgotten about the deadline for voluntary withdrawals.

**SAVITRI:** Beta, finish that degree. Just a few weeks of work and it will be over.

**VITHAL:** Does it matter?

**SAVITRI:** The degree itself doesn't. But completing something you've started does. Let's make a deal. You write the exams, and I'll. . . .

**VITHAL:** Exams and courses aren't the problem, kaku.

**SAVITRI:** Donna? How's Donna?

**VITHAL:** *(Distantly)* Oh, that's been off a long time.

**SAVITRI:** Something that's been on for five years can't be turned off that easily.

**VITHAL:** It wasn't easy.

**SAVITRI:** I can't believe Donna would break it off. I know her. She's devoted to you.

**VITHAL:** *She* didn't.

**SAVITRI:** Beta! You? Why would you do that? Donna is one in a million.

**VITHAL:** *(Bitterly)* But I'm a dime a dozen. A habitual dropout, a drag. And she is halfway to being a doctor.

**SAVITRI:** Stop belittling yourself. You have the Midas touch, Vithal, but you refuse to touch anything. Any and every thing you do would be done superlatively well but you drop it without ever trying. Maybe you aren't into the university program. Get back to RRCC and finish one of the courses you started last year.

**VITHAL:** And become a cruddy electrician? Or would you rather I finish the masonry course! Or the plumbing?

**SAVITRI:** It would make no difference to us. And it would make no difference to Donna. I know her.

**VITHAL:** I believe it, kaku. You'll love me as much, but you'd still wish I'd chosen to touch something else with my Midas touch. Donna too. She'll love me, sure, and so would any children we might have, so would they all, all honourable men. But I have neither wit nor words. . . . Deep down, way down she would have that core of disappointment. A basic imbalance. . . . A professional woman has certain fundamental standards, expectations.

**SAVITRI:** You are being unfair to her. In personal relationships that one makes with open eyes, one. . . .

**VITHAL:** We'll start off with the best of intentions, don't doubt that. But she will go on, zooming ahead, and just give up on me after a while.

**SAVITRI:** Donna is more Hindu than many of us.

**VITHAL:** I don't doubt it. She'd never divorce me, indeed, we'd be a great couple from the outside, especially if I kept away from a full-time profession. But the core, at the core something would be missing. A woman, even a Hindu-like woman, maybe especially a Hindu-like woman, expects her man to be up there, higher than herself, and woe to the man who can't be a demigod. All the other men they will sympathize with, and even admire, but their own man? Oh, no, he has to be some kind of a titan. Ain't I right? Ain't I?

**SAVITRI:** Get up there, Vithal, you can climb to the top of any ladder you want. Why don't you do something new? Join politics. It is time we had some of our people there. Your Desh Hall friends, isn't that what they say?

**VITHAL:** I don't go there any more. *(Again his voice is dispirited, but this time he does not rally from the silence that follows. Then he speaks slowly.)* You can do all these controversial, way out things only when you are basically happy. If I get into a violent situation now, and that comes naturally at the Desh Hall, even if it were exactly what I've been doing forever, everyone would promptly trace it to a broken home or a broken affair or whatever. *(In silence Jyoti and Savitri continue to move about from counter to table to refrigerator.)*

**SAVITRI:** Veejala was to have lunch with me at school yesterday but didn't turn up. Last Monday she phoned and postponed the lunch to yesterday, but this time she didn't even phone.

**VITHAL:** *(Getting up)* She needs you. *(More softly)* I guess we all do. *(He goes down.)*

**JYOTI:** *(Slowly, fearfully)* Is something the matter?

**SAVITRI:** He's always been a moody boy, how was he before I came?

**JYOTI:** *(More relaxed)* His usual self, I thought. Talking nonstop. With more gusto, if anything, because he had a captive audience in this boy who's just come from Delhi. The usual high; you know Vithal, about "we have the same rights as these pissed-off whites, we'll build a temple on the Red and Assiniboine," and all that stuff we've heard a hundred times.

**SAVITRI:** *(Quietly)* Yet every time I hear him, I am moved by those words. Even though I don't feel the same way. Some day, I hope, Vithal and all of you will realize that we have already built that temple because we carry our gods within us and with us wherever we go.

**JYOTI:** *(Fearful again)* What did he say about auntie? What did he mean? Tell me, mom, what's happening?

**SAVITRI:** *(Reassuringly calm)* Veejala has always been a rebel. I don't think I've told you of the pandemonium she created soon after my wedding. I came to know later that it was only one of many, but it was a storm such as I'd never known in my father's house. She sold her diamond ring so she could enrol in an aviation course; the family had said no, and so she went right ahead and got the money anyway. The ring was a family heirloom, given by Peshwa Balaji Rao, and you can imagine the furore. She has done some wonderfully crazy things, as you know.

**JYOTI:** *(Admiringly)* She's neat. Always on the go, stunning every which way, looks, confidence.

**SAVITRI:** She makes it so very difficult for one to excuse her actions, but I have always found it even more difficult not to.

**JYOTI:** She's a sloppy housewife, though. Poor Vithal, I am sure, hasn't had a good meal in ages. All the puris and raita were his idea.

**SAVITRI:** Vee was never much of a housewife. Back home she was used to returning from work and finding a hot dinner ready, clothes washed, the house spic and span; it hasn't been easy to adjust.

**JYOTI:** *(Stung into a kind of jealousy)* But she's been here a lot longer than you and—

**SAVITRI:** *(In a reminiscing voice)* That flat they had in Delhi when they returned from the States. Fabulous gadgets we had seen only in pictures. Electric range, toaster, oven, washing machine . . . and a fleet of servants too.

**JYOTI:** Oh, mom, beat it, she has hired help here too. If anything, you are the one who's got a bad deal. Granddad's house, wow, what a mansion, and here you are working your fingers to the bone, scrubbing and polishing. *(With sudden passion)* I'll start hating this place the day your hands lose their softness.

**SAVITRI:** They'll survive, beti, they'll survive, but will our spirits? No matter how long we live here, it is never long enough to forget either our old ways or our old comforts.

**JYOTI:** *(Laughing indulgently)* Mom, you've just finished saying we carry our temple within us, and now this. There's consistency for you.

**SAVITRI:** *(Laughing)* Is that inconsistent? You youngsters corner us at every turn. I don't know, Jyotishma, I used to believe that if only I could take time out from housework and school to think, I could sort out all the questions, iron out all the inconsistencies and find out what life is all about. But I have never really tried to make time. I suppose I am afraid of the answers. What if there's no pot of gold at the end of the rainbow? So we take up more chores than we can handle and we make sure we never have leisure enough to think. It works well most of the time but those few times we are faced with some brutal truth, we panic, we just can't cope, and we lash out at each other.

*She looks at Jyoti, who looks back. They stand a moment, their eyes locked in understanding and compassion. and they simultaneously get back to work.*

## Scene IV

*Afternoon, Savitri is drinking tea as in Scene III of Act One. Sharad enters, his face flushed and upset. He comes in and thuds onto a chair. He takes off his gloves but not his parka. His boots make a slow puddle at his feet as the scene progresses.*

**SHARAD:** What is this about Veejal? Why didn't you tell me all these days?

**SAVITRI:** What did she say? Would you like some tea? *(She moves as though to get up.)*

**SHARAD:** No, I am shaking all over. It is a wonder I managed to drive home without an accident. *(He wipes his forehead, which is sweating.)* Now tell me.

**SAVITRI:** I doubt I know any more than you do. What did she tell you?

**SHARAD:** When I came back to the office an hour ago, there was a message asking me to call her back. She had called just before ten, Marie said.

**SAVITRI:** You've had a long day.

**SHARAD:** Yes, Mrs Pringle's deal has come through, and the way the market is standing still these days, it is cause enough to celebrate, but God *(He wipes himself)* I called her back and she was as cool as cool can be. Said she had already resigned her job and was going back home. That she wanted to tell me herself so I wouldn't come to know of it secondhand from someone else. And that was all. No reason, nothing. And I couldn't very well ask her any questions, you know how our office cubicles are. Why did she do it? Who is she going with? Do you know him?

**SAVITRI:** Why do you assume she's going with someone?

**SHARAD:** Why else would any woman leave her husband and home? And the way you are taking it, I am sure you know a lot more of what is happening but you won't give it away. Please, please tell me. At her age, too, gods help us. She's crazy. *(He looks at Savitri, waiting for her to speak but she says nothing.)*

**SHARAD:** *(Now hurt more than angry)* How could she? Without telling us anything at all. Why did I choose this godforsaken eternal winter of a place, except so we could foster a sense of family even though so far from home? Just to be near her so we'd have each other to turn to in time of need. But she never came, never asked for help. *(He is deeply moved)* She always came to me. Not to Mukund or Hari but always to me. Whether it was to take a sliver from her finger or to help in her arithmetic homework, always she knew she could trust me. Any boy father selected for her, she wanted me to meet him first. Bhau, she'd say, never mind looks, never mind money, make sure, absolutely sure that he won't stand in the way of my studies, she'd say each time. She relied on me and I carried out her trust. And now, *(He holds his head in his hands.)* and now. . . . *(Angry)* How could she? Tell me, Savi, you know the story. I'm sure you do. Who is he?

**SAVITRI:** There is no one else.

**SHARAD:** Did you ask her?

**SAVITRI:** There isn't.

**SHARAD:** So you didn't ask.

**SAVITRI:** How little you know your sister!

**SHARAD:** *(Bitterly)* How little we know anyone. Veejala, my little sister who wouldn't choose her Divali sari without consulting me, leaves her husband and children for some crazy goon.

**SAVITRI:** Stop jumping to conclusions. There isn't anyone else. She told me.

**SHARAD:** She did?

**SAVITRI:** Yes she did, but that is the only thing she told me. She didn't tell me why she was doing what she was doing.

**SHARAD:** *(Relieved)* Going home for a holiday is fine. We can always take care of Pixie. *(Worried)* But why didn't she come down and tell us in person instead of exploding such a bombshell over the phone? And why did she have to resign her job? *(Upset again)* How could anyone be so imprudent as to give up a job? With all the cutbacks and retrenchments, doesn't she know she can never get it back? She could have taken leave. They'd be only too glad to let her go on loss of salary. I could have advised her, if she had so much as given a hint that she was contemplating something so ridiculous. Did she talk it over with Anant?

**SAVITRI:** Anant knows.

**SHARAD:** You are hiding something, Savi.

**SAVITRI:** I am not hiding anything. I just don't see any point in repeating certain things. *(She makes as though to get up but then changes her mind and pours herself another cup of tea. She speaks slowly, deliberately.)* I asked her if she had discussed it with him and she replied that they still spent hours discussing their social schedule—what parties to give and to go to—but that for years they had merely told each other their major decisions; they never talked things over.

**SHARAD:** *(Who has winced at this, speaks hesitantly)* Are you sure there is no one else, that Anant. . . .

**SAVITRI:** *(Smiling sympathetically at Sharad's discomfiture)* Anant? I wonder if we aren't being brainwashed by our environment?—that we can think only of illicit relationships at the root of all troubles. I don't know what Veejala's problem is. We know she does crazy things, but her sense of morality is even more puritanical than mine—the morality she sets up for herself, I mean. I only hope that isn't harming her.

**SHARAD:** Meaning?

**SAVITRI:** Never mind. I am content to wait until she is ready to tell me more.

**SHARAD:** *(Now much calmer)* Maybe I will have some tea. Let me get the newspapers. *(He goes out and returns with the newspapers.)*

**SAVITRI:** What news of the flood?

**SHARAD:** Nothing to add to the morning's news. The crest is expected fourth or fifth instead of the seventh. *(He is turning over the pages.)* Oh no! That is why she was in such a rush to tell us!

**SAVITRI:** What's up?

**SHARAD:** Oh no! Photograph and all!

**SAVITRI:** *(Leans over his shoulder and reads aloud parts of the news story, her face showing admiration and delight while Sharad holds his head in his hands and groans.)* "University professor quits backwoods of Canada for backwoods of India. . . . Dr Veejala Moghe, assistant professor of astronomy, has resigned her faculty position . . . claims this is a backwood . . . where nothing of significance has been done or can be done in her faculty. . . . Dr Moghe plans to spend the summer at the Pasadena Observatory of the University of California before leaving for her native India. . . . Asked if conditions were any better in India, she said they were not, but she would feel better wasting her life in her native country than wasting it in the backwoods of Canada. 'This place doesn't exist on any academic map,' she said, 'but my name does, and I'd rather not atrophy here.' . . . who has published extensively in her field and is a Fellow of the Royal Astronomical Society, was asked why her work had not been recognized at this university. She replied she had never bothered to push herself politically. . . . Asked if she felt she had been discriminated against because of her sex, Dr Moghe said, 'I happen to be of the wrong colour as well.'"

**SHARAD:** Oh God, if she wanted to go, why couldn't she just go quietly instead of drawing us all in? What has she said about Anant and the children?

**SAVITRI:** Nothing much. Just straight facts. Here, read it.

**SHARAD:** *(Pushing away the newspaper)* Not now. My head is splitting.

*Savitri takes the newpaper off the table and reads the news story again, smiling appreciatively.*

## ACT THREE

### Scene I

*Lunch hour. Savitri is setting the table for two. Veejala comes in. She is a strikingly good-looking woman in her early forties. Her black hair, waved back, cascades down her shoulders, half-way down her back; she is taller than Savitri, and is wearing an expensive pantsuit and heeled snowboots. Elegant and poised when still, she has masculine confidence when she speaks; the flash of her eyes and the way she blinks deeply are due partly to arrogance and partly to longsightedness. Savitri embraces her warmly. Veejala sits at the table while the soup boils, and plugs in the coffeepot.*

**VEEJALA:** I am sorry to be a little late; the traffic never seems to let up on Fridays.

**SAVITRI:** Don't worry. I've taken the afternoon off.

**VEEJALA:** You have! At such short notice? Old man Grierson won't like it.

**SAVITRI:** He doesn't know. Beverly will manage to get a sub. Anyway, I deserve a break. I haven't called in sick or taken leave in ages, not since Krish cracked his forehead last May and I was called to Emergency.

**VEEJALA:** You make me feel as though I was dying or something. Taking the day off for my emergency.

**SAVITRI:** Some people think it is.

**VEEJALA:** Sharad! Poor bhau, I suppose he's frantic with anxiety.

**SAVITRI:** He was at first. Now he's moved toward anger, I think.

**VEEJALA:** I thought he'd be anxious. He always was rather protective about me. I must say I'm disappointed.

**SAVITRI:** It is hard to worry about you, Vee. You know that all too well. People like to be needed. For some people, the best gift you can give is to ask them for help. But you. . . .

**VEEJALA:** Yes, it is such an irony that bhau is stuck in this hole. He should be back in Poona, presiding over the family in the mansion—zamindar, dispenser of ancestral wealth, friend of the lessee peasants, godfather to all the village brats who want to get a college education. *(Pushes away the soup that Savitri has placed in front of her.)* No offence, Savi, but I can't down anything. What I need is whiskey, neat, but I don't suppose you'd have it.

**SAVITRI:** Shall I make you some masala tea?

**VEEJALA:** You should be there, too. Flapping your shapely bum in a nine-yard sari, Annapurni, generous hostess, brewing masala tea for sore throats and aching hearts.

**SAVITRI:** If anyone needs to be there, it is you. You could puff away at a cigarette and stomp around in your shorts or bikinis and you'd have gotten the rebel out of your system for a while. Here you have to kill yourself to prove a point, because nothing short of that is rebellion. *(They look at each other across the table.)*

**VEEJALA:** Why are we being so crabby to each other?

**SAVITRI:** *(Swallowing the tears in her eyes and smiling)* Because.

**VEEJALA:** *(Leaning forward intensely)* Don't you know why I did it? Don't you understand?

**SAVITRI:** No.

**VEEJALA:** I d hoped you would, at least you.

**SAVITRI:** There are many things about you I don't understand, Vee, but that has never come between us.

**VEEJALA:** *(Quietly)* And this has?

**SAVITRI:** *(Quietly)* No, it hasn't. Perhaps it should, but it hasn't.

**VEEJALA:** But you don t approve.

**SAVITRI:** I don't know. I've always held that when an essentially moral person does something usually considered immoral, it is more likely to have moral reasons than immoral.

**VEEJALA:** But in this, you don't?

**SAVITRI:** I don't know, Vee, I don't know. What can I say except the usual things. That at least for the children's sake. . . .

**VEEJALA:** The children don't need me. A child grows as a flower grows.

**SAVITRI:** But it grows better when there is sunshine and there aren't weeds. *(Shakes her head)* No, it is so hard not to fall into cliches.

**VEEJALA:** Because this is a cliche situation? A woman walking out on her husband? *(Savitri shakes her head)* Okay, okay.

*(Veejala leans her elbow on the table and presses her forehead and speaks slowly.)* The children. They are not really ours. They are their own, and all too soon they realize that. When Vithal went off that summer, I missed him, oh, how I missed him, and yet when he came back, everything was changed. He was his own world, set in his ways, self-contained, the umbilical cord broken off. Everything seemed the same, but it wasn't. I wonder if that's how our mothers felt when we got married. I remember my first visit at rakhi time the autumn I got married. Oh, I was so happy to be back, it was like rolling back into the niche where I belonged. And yet, maybe it wasn't so to mother. Come to think of it, I was pampered and indulged in, an honoured guest. That's probably how mother felt about me, just as I felt about Vithal. A pain, an excruciating pain where the cord had been pulled off, deep, deep in the guts, but something final. No, it is not the children I will miss or worry about. . . . I have always been something of a magpie. It is Anant. Already I feel as though I've left half my self behind. . . . But it is a half that is best left behind. *(Silence for a moment)*

**SAVITRI:** It is the suddenness of it all. Even I didn't know it was coming. One could see the problems, of course, the incompatibilities, that others wouldn't have. But then every marriage, every job has some of that. And we haven't had more than the usual share. So why?

**VEEJALA:** That's not it, that's not it at all. I don't know, Savi. It is my turn to say that.

**SAVITRI:** Maybe you are still just a spoiled brat.

**VEEJALA:** Maybe. Or maybe it is my last desperate attempt to do something worthwhile. Instead of being tied down to a bloodless rat race. Twenty-five thousand a year and no sweat to speak of. A handsome scientist for a husband and two lovely children. An eighty-thousand-dollar house and the whole works. Everything one could ever wish for. And yet when I look through that telescope and see the stars, when I watch the shimmering dance of Borealis, I feel I have to go have one last crack at real scholarship. Leave everything and follow me, he said, and right away Simon, who was called Peter, left everything and followed him.

*Phone rings. Savitri picks it up.*

**SAVITRI:** I am feeling better, thanks, Bev. Any problems? Yes, Mr Grierson. . . . Did you try Cindy? She's usually home at lunch time. . . . Well, they are working on their project for the first hour and. . . . I suppose I could come out for the last two classes. . . . No, I am sorry there is no way I can get myself out for the first hour. . . . Yes I'll be there. *(Hangs up)*

**VEEJALA:** Sucker, every time a sucker, Savi. I know. I heard. You have to go. You are so unrelentingly sweet.

**SAVITRI:** *(Smiling)* So unrelentingly stupid, that is all. I think everyone should be taught how to tell a lie. It is as essential as knowing how to fall the right way in hockey or football. But you take your time, Vee, rest for a while.

**VEEJALA:** Don't worry about me. Get back to your sheep.

*Savitri hastily finishes her lunch and starts clearing away the table.*

**VEEJALA:** *(To herself more than to Savitri)* I am not young. I can't concentrate even an hour on anything I read. My eyes are half gone. And I haven't churned out even my usual quota of papers these two years . . . throwing away a pearl of great price for something glowing in the dark that could well be a leopard's eyes staring at the kill.

## Scene II

*Same scene as before. Veejala is at the table, coffee mug and several magazines in front of her. She has her legs up on the chair across. Sunlight streams in from the left. Jyoti is taking off her boots.*

**JYOTI:** *(Guardedly)* Hullo, auntie.

**VEEJALA:** Hullo, Jyu!

**JYOTI:** Been here long? Had lunch?

**VEEJALA:** Yes, thanks, you?

**JYOTI:** Sort of. Mom home?

**VEEJALA:** No, she was here but now she's back at work. I should be going too. Have a 3:40 class. *(Jyoti helps herself to a pop from the refrigerator.)*

**VEEJALA:** How are things? How's Andre?

**JYOTI:** *(Distantly)* He's alright, thanks.

**VEEJALA:** None of my business, in other words.

**JYOTI:** *(Her back turned to Veejala as she opens a cabinet for a glass.)* It is your business, auntie, just as it is mine to ask you what is happening. But we've lost the ability to ask and answer.

**VEEJALA:** *(After a moment's silence)* We are lucky as long as we can have one or two to whom we can still talk.

**JYOTI:** If. But everything burns up one's hand. You feel real close to someone and then bang slam, the door shuts on your face. *(Jyoti turns as if to go away, but then sits at the table, back to the sun.)* Sridhar, I thought I could really talk to him.

**VEEJALA:** We are all pretty dumb at times, Jyu, but surely you are not so dumb that you didn't know he was head over heels in love with you?

**JYOTI:** I could talk to him, I really could.

**VEEJALA:** One can never talk to the ones closest to oneself.

**JYOTI:** I didn't know he was that close to me. I guess I was misled by his insistence that I was. Anyway, it is all far too confusing right now. Let's talk about you. *(She is more relaxed.)*

**VEEJALA:** What makes you think that's any less confusing?

**JYOTI:** You've taken action. One can't come to that without having resolved the confusion.

**VEEJALA:** It could be that one takes action thinking one has resolved it. But then one might find oneself still confused. Hasn't that happened to you? After you first made love, for instance?

**JYOTI:** *(Angrily)* Mom has—

**VEEJALA:** Certainly not. Savi hasn't told me anything.

**JYOTI:** *(Sarcastically)* Just a shot in the dark.

**VEEJALA:** And you were dumb enough to give yourself away.

**JYOTI:** It shows in my eyes, eh? The sparkle of stars and all that.

**VEEJALA:** More in one's hips after a while, I believe. Mine was a shot in the dark. But those aunts and great aunts back home, they developed some kind of sixth sense, maybe. I wish I had picked up some of the tidbits of knowledge teenagers pick up just listening to those women. *(She goes on reminiscently.)* They didn't miss anything, I can tell you, even though they seldom left the house compound. I remember how Kamal . . . well, I won't bore you with old tales. Sign of old age. Must guard myself against that, eh! Frankly, I simply assumed you were no virgin. It is the tight-lipped type that gives in, the so-called loose ones who let themselves be patted and stroked by one and all hang on to their virginity a lot longer. *(Jyoti is close to tears. Veejala notices it, gets up impulsively, and embraces her.)*

**VEEJALA:** That was mean of me, Jyu, I am sorry. And ashamed. Treating you like a grown-up. I am on your side, Jyoti; it is a beautiful experience, quite quite ravishing, shall we say? *(She kisses Jyoti on the forehead and strokes her hair.)* It will be very confusing for a while even without the gossip. And gossip will be hard to take. Everyone will say you are a fool to choose a long-haired, hip-type foreigner when you have a clean-cut intelligent Hindu waiting on you. But tell them that if this were India, their counterparts would be saying the same thing about Sridhar the alien southerner; oh, oh, there I go again, assumed like an old fogie that you were planning to marry one of them. You don't have to, Jyoti. Sharad would kill me if he heard me give you this advice, but it is as sound a piece of advice for anyone living today in this country—jump into bed as many times as you wish, but don't jump into matrimony. We, born and brought up in another age and another culture, know that marriage is for keeps, and we are willing to make a million adjustments, but you kids who grow up here are so rigid in your expectations, so lax in your commitment, you throw in the towel the minute something goes wrong. Your uncle and I would have been divorced a dozen times if we hadn't the background we have. Both of us have been outrageously irresponsible; I've done the craziest things when we had money, and you know about most of them; and he's been the reason we never had much money for the first million years we were students. Why do you think it took me ten years to get my degree? I was working at odd jobs—library, dish-washing, waitressing, in addition to my assistantship, anything I could get. . . .

**JYOTI:** You were? You mean you were poor?

**VEEJALA:** As a churchmouse.

**JYOTI:** But why?

**VEEJALA:** Ah, there were reasons, my love. Those were great times, Jyoti. Such experiences as few can have. We were both A-plus students. And crazy. One has to be a little crazy if one is to do anything worthwhile. My first paper, back in '61, was quite something. Pasadena, that's why I am going there, Pasadena was my starting point. I was shaking like a leaf the whole time I was presenting the paper, and a very pregnant leaf, too. I wanted to go back to my room and sleep, but then there were questions and discussions on the paper that went on longer than I've ever seen. As soon as I could get away I ran to our room and threw up. That was some scene. Vithal, open mouthed and ready to bawl, Anant frantic, and who should knock? Professor Steiner, come to congratulate me. Steiner in person, and me doubled up over the washbasin. '61, wonderful, sad '61.

**JYOTI:** You lost the baby right then?

**VEEJALA:** No, two weeks later, back home, thank God. You needn't look so commiserating, Jyu, I couldn't have cared less at the time. Success was so heady, so absobloominutely great, it was a fair bargain—recognition in exchange for a five-month-old foetus. I got seventy-three requests for copies of my paper that first year. A fair and square bargain dealt out by fate. You have to pay a price for everything and I've never regretted that. But now, what am I getting for the high price of inertia that I am paying? There was no answer to that. Which is why I am striking out.

**JYOTI:** Pasadena, London, Delhi, it sounds exciting and wonderful. And *(Hesitantly)* so reassuring to know that you are not breaking up with Uncle Anant for . . . just for the breaking up.

**VEEJALA:** You would like to be really sure of that, wouldn't you? *(Jyoti nods, half eager, half afraid. Veejala draws her head to her breast.)* We are all in one godamnawful mess, my love, but still lucky; we have one or two we can hold on to. And now I am going to rest for a few minutes in Savi's ever ready guestroom. *(Exits)*

*Lights dim and immediately go up on the same scene. There is no one in the kitchen, but Jyoti and Andre are talking offstage on the back landing. Their shadows dance on the kitchen wall.*

**JYOTI:** *(Her voice is still calm but a little louder than usual)* Not this week, Andre, please don't pester me.

**ANDRE:** *(Loud and angry)* Pester you! I've been away almost a week, and you refuse me a date.

**JYOTI:** Oh, Andre, please don't ask me. I missed you, missed you so much. If only you didn't have to go, if you hadn't gone, maybe. . . .

**ANDRE:** Maybe what? Come on, honey bun, just a couple of hours.

**JYOTI:** *(With quiet firmness)* No, Andre, no. I could give you half a dozen reasons. I am working all week evenings, I have two final exams coming up, mom's car has to go to the garage, all true, but they aren't the reason. It is me. I am confused. I have to sort things out.

**ANDRE:** What things? You said the same thing over the phone. What d'you mean. I have a car, love.

**JYOTI:** Things, you and me. I need time.

**ANDRE:** Damn it, how can you be so cool, so rational. One day I'll get into your inner kernel of stillness. I swear I will tear my way into that silence and hear you scream of lust and pain. God, you stand there as though nothing moves you, but I know, goddamnit, I know you are a cauldron of emotions sealed four times over. *(Sound of back door slamming. Jyoti comes in and takes her place at the window. Veejala comes in.)*

**JYOTI:** I didn't think you could have heard.

**VEEJALA:** Not hear a tornado? What in you brings out such violence, Jyoti? I grant you are not quite the average kid next door, but this, oof.

**JYOTI:** What do you think I should be feeling?

**VEEJALA:** Hm. I think you should be thrilled to pieces, to use Pixie's phrase, to have aroused such a passion in someone.

**JYOTI:** I am nothing. Just a blank wall or mirror or something. Each one sees himself in me. I have nothing to do with anything they feel. I am just nothing in myself. Maybe that's why I arouse violence. . . . And yet, the other day I felt so warm and today I feel so distant.

**VEEJALA:** We are far too serious about everything. Why don't we just laugh, roll around in the snow, build a snowcastle.

**JYOTI:** *(Intensely)* May I come with you to India? I've always wanted to travel around India. It seems so far away, so blurred, even though I was eleven or twelve when we left. Please.

**VEEJALA:** *(Lightly)* I'd have said yes right away if I hadn't heard the cyclone shooting through. To tell you the truth, Jyoti, I have regretted that miscarriage. It was a girl. I've burned with envy a million times, love, seeing you and Savitri together. And the only reason I haven't wooed you closer to myself is because I know how much I want you there. So maybe I'd have refused to take you even sans cyclone.

**JYOTI:** Say that again. I lost you.

**VEEJALA:** Never mind. Now that I heard all this thunder, I have to say that you have to face up to your problems, you can't run away from them, not with me nowise. I'll let you in on another secret, Jyoti; for several years I've wanted to quit and strike out as I'm doing now, but things weren't quite right between Anant and myself. And if I'd left then, I might have felt guilty all the time that I was running away from something that I perhaps did not want rather than going toward something I want with all my soul. But now all is fine between us.

**JYOTI:** Do you really have to go? Vithal needs you.

**VEEJALA:** Anyone else would have said Priti needs me. But you know me better.

**JYOTI:** Vithal is only an excuse. I need you. Please.

**VEEJALA:** We are all in one godawful mess, my darling, but we'll survive.

## Scene III

*Basement. Savitri is ironing, Jyoti is folding Savitri's colourful saris.*

**SAVITRI:** Don't think I haven't recognized your contempt for us who have been faithful all our lives, Jyoti. It hurts, but I know that too is a form of idealism—to think that love is free, not to be bound. . . . And I believe love is free. . . . Love makes one beautiful, so so breathtakingly beautiful. Your cousin Kanta, I remember when her mother was in love. That was my first experience of love, it was at second hand, of course, as first experiences often are. She was staying with us that year, going to college. It was one of my best years because when someone is in love she can give and receive affection so purely, so spontaneously, that the happiness keeps spreading in concentric circles, drawing more and more people into itself. Oh, she was beautiful. . . .

**JYOTI:** What happened then?

**SAVITRI:** What happens to so many girls. There was a big hullaballoo and she was married off to a rich widower who lived so far away he couldn't have heard any of this gossip. She's spent her life milking cows and supervising the measuring of the harvest. But *(Her eyes shine with remembrance)* she had it, Jyoti, for only a few months, but she had the real thing. That is why I feel so much for you, for your sadness.

**JYOTI:** *(Softly)* It is not the real thing, is that what it means?

**SAVITRI:** *(After a pause)* If I were sure of that, I would tell you so.

**JYOTI:** I don't want to believe it, mom, first love, it is my first love. *(Her voice breaks.)*

*Savitri pauses in her ironing and looks at her. But Jyoti has already recovered.*

**JYOTI:** *(In normal voice)* I think you've missed this part. It needs to be redone.

**SAVITRI:** *(Taking the sari from her, she says half seriously, half jokingly)* Never consummate your first love, and you'll have it all your life. Mother Philomena used to say it at the end-of-the-ear counselling to us.

**JYOTI:** *(Casually)* Did you have one, mom?

**SAVITRI:** *(Laughing)* Now, now, Jyoti, how am I supposed to answer that? If I say I didn't, I'd plummet down in your esteem! *(Points her thumb downward.)*

**JYOTI:** And if you said you did?

**SAVITRI:** Probably I would plummet down sometime later.

**JYOTI:** We need to know, mom, we've got to know more about our parents. We never do. I've sometimes wondered, mom, wondered in what senseless moment of upward kicking of legs and flailing arms I was conceived.

**SAVITRI:** *(Matter-of-factly)* Would it help if I said you were conceived in the springtime of my love, in the floodtide of desire? It is true, but would it really help? As for knowing about one's parents, we don't need facts. My parents were so different, now that I see their personalities from my experience I see so much more, but when I was a child, a girl, even a young woman, I naturally and blindly believed my parents were an open book to one another, that there was no secret anywhere.

**JYOTI:** But that 's how I see you and dad!

**SAVITRI:** All is not lost, my munchkin. One day may you be as happy as I have been.

## Scene IV

*Phone rings. Jyoti enters from the back door at the fourth ring. She has just come in from the outside—she has on her winter coat and boots. In the ensuing scene, Jyoti speaks into the kitchen phone while on the other side of the stage Sridhar is speaking from a telephone booth.*

**JYOTI:** Hullo.

**SRIDHAR:** Hullo, Jyoti.

**JYOTI:** Hi, Sri. Wait a sec while I take off my coat. I've just come in.

**SRIDHAR:** I know. I saw you.

**JYOTI:** Saw me? Where?

**SRIDHAR:** As you turned off King s Drive.

**JYOTI:** And you didn't bother to give me a ride. Boy, some folks can be mean.

**SRIDHAR:** Would you have accepted?

**JYOTI:** *(Evading the question)* What were you doing there at this time of day?

**SRIDHAR:** Following you.

*Jyoti's colour rises. She opens her mouth as though to say something, but her lips tremble and she says nothing.*

**SRIDHAR:** *(His voice less strained now)* You didn't think all those "chance encounters" over the last year were accidental, did you? I made an ass of myself the other day. I've been slapping myself ever since. So suicidal of me, to blast the ground from under my feet. I suppose that's the end? *(The last question is in a very low, strained voice.)*

*Jyoti doesn't reply.*

**SRIDHAR:** I've been going over those few minutes ever since. When I started spouting my great rhetoric, there was a moment when I could have stopped myself. But I went on, quite sure it would do me good to get it out of my system. God, what an ass. *(Jyoti does not reply but there are tears gathering in her eyes.)* We can't meet on the same footing any more . . . can we?

**JYOTI:** No.

**SRIDHAR:** Quoth the raven, Nevermore. *(He tries to sound flippant.)*

**JYOTI:** *(Slowly)* Not on that footing but maybe, maybe on. . . .

**SRIDHAR:** *(Incredulous and overjoyed)* Jyoti! *(More his usual* *self.)* You mean you haven't thrown me out on my ear? That we can, we might, with a bit of amnesia, talk again? May I come over now?

**JYOTI:** *(Her eyes clearer now)* Hey, hey, not so fast.

*She disconnects the call with her free hand and stands cradling the receiver, running her fingers over the mouthpiece as lights dim.*

## Scene V

*Jayant is having a Coke at the kitchen table . The phone rings.*

**JAYANT:** *(Picking up the receiver)* Hullo.

**PRITI:** *(At the other end)* Jai? Oh, Jaida, thank God you are home. *(Panic and relief come through clearly in her voice as she speaks.)*

**JAYANT:** *(With concern and tenderness on his face but in a normal, special voice)* Hi! Pixie Trix! Whassa matta? Boogeyman a-chasing you? Wanna Big Brave to rescue you?

**PRITI:** Oh Jai, can you pick us up? We are stranded.

**JAYANT:** Where? What do you mean "we"? Who?

**PRITI:** At Polo Park, Laura and me. Mommy was to pick us up at 5:30 but she hasn't come.

**JAYANT:** *(Under his breath.)*Jeesus. It is 6:20!

**PRITI:** And she hasn't come yet. And the stores are all closed and the people all gone.

**JAYANT:** *(To himself angrily)* God, how irresponsible can one get? She doesn't deserve to have kids. *(To Priti soothingly)* Chin up, bebe. Where are you now?

**PRITI:** Near Eaton's. Just where mommy told us to be.

**JAYANT:** Walk back through the mall to the door near Sears.

**PRITI:** But mommy told us to wait here. Why hasn't she come. *(In tears)* She said she would.

**JAYANT:** You know how mommy has a hundred and thirty-nine things on her mind twenty-eight hours a day, Pixie. Both of you go to the Sears door—the Bread and Key entrance, get it?

Near the cinema. And stay between the doors. And don't worry. People will soon be coming to the movie. And store managers will soon be coming out, too, from every store. And there will be people at the bus stop, get it? And listen, even if your mum does turn up, don't take off. Stay on until I come down. Clear? Go straight to the cinema place and stay put. I'll be there in twenty minutes. Got a watch?

**PRITI:** Laura has hers.

**JAYANT:** Good, remember I can't reach you till twenty minutes from now. Take a look at the watch now, else you'll think it is an hour after five minutes.

**PRITI:** Okay, shall I hang up?

**JAYANT:** K.O. Pixie-Trix. *(Hangs up, checks that he has his car keys in his pocket, and rushes out without a coat.)*

## Scene VI

*An hour later. Jayant comes in, followed by Priti and Laura, whose chattering voices precede them. Priti runs through the kitchen and comes back with a volume of* Brittanica.

**PRITI:** Here. There's twenty pages of stuff on Egypt here. Enough for two projects.

**JAYANT:** Sit down, Laura, I am going to make some hot chocolate for all of us.

**LAURA:** No thanks, I am late for dinner as it is. Thanks for the ride, Jai. And bye, Priti. *(Pronounces it "Pretty.")* I'll return this tomorrow.

**PRITI:** I don't need that volume for my project. Keep it as long as you want to. *(Laura leaves. Jayant warms milk in a saucepan and takes out a can of Quik. Priti sits at the table; suddenly she bursts out crying, head buried in her arms.)*

**PRITI:** *(Sobbing )* What am I going to do? What am I gonna do?

**JAYANT:** What's eating ma petite princess?

**PRITI:** Three times this week I was late to school. And today she forgot altogether.

**JAYANT:** Just a rough patch, munchkin. You know all about life under a volcano. A rumble here, a tremor there. But you should be used to it by now. Come on, take it easy.

**PRITI:** Three days. You don't know Miss Grindley. Takes a ratch even for no reason. And you know the school rules. Three times late and you are finished. You don't know our school.

**JAYANT:** I thought you liked this school. Your mum was praising it so much. Said you enjoyed it.

**PRITI:** Now I know why she put me there. Cos we have a residence. That's why. So she can leave me and not have to worry about me when there is no home left.

**JAYANT:** *(Angrily)* Bull *(He pauses.)*—y for you. *(Tenderly)* What's this if not your home, you silly goose. Next year you shall stay right here. And meanwhile I shall drive you to school every morning.

**PRITI:** *(Taking it as a game)* Promise by the hair on your chinny chinny chin?

**JAYANT:** Promise by the hair on my chinny chinny chin.

**PRITI:** Cross your heart and hope to die?

**JAYANT:** Cross my heart and hope to die.

**PRITI:** *(Totally relaxed)* Sounds good, Jai. Only one teeny weeny snag. You're leaving.

**JAYANT:** Can't. I've promised to be your chauffeur.

**PRITI:** *(Handing him an imaginary paper)* Here, take back your promise. I don't want to stop you from making your fortune in your seven league boots.

**JAYANT:** Can't. A promise is a promise is a kick in the butt if I break it.

**PRITI:** You shouldn't upset all your plans for a silly little problem like mine. I can take the bus. Even if I do have to get up at 6:30 to get to that stupid bus that always leaves just as ours reaches the corner. But *(Plaintively)* I wish mommy wouldn't say she'd take me; then I get up late and she gets up late anyway and by the time we leave . . . she thinks it is okay to be a few minutes late, but it isn't. We just have to be in by 8:45. We just have to. *(She is close to tears again.)*

**JAYANT:** Eight o'clock every morning now to the end of June. I'll pick you up on the dot of eight, and if you aren't ready, oh boy, you'll get it from me, forget Miss Grouchy.

**PRITI:** *(Laughing)* Grindley.

**JAYANT:** Whatever. But keep it a secret for now. I'll come Monday morning and we'll spill it then, okay?

**PRITI:** But you are all set to go!

**JAYANT:** I'll stay. If there's a Christly chance for me to do something for someone, I'd gladly stay put. Jeesus, how dispensable we are. I'd stay even if that stupid parakeet of yours said it needed me to clean its cage. How much more readily for you. . . . Here, a glutton aren't you? Didn't leave a drop for me. *(Takes up the saucepan and turns it upside down.)*

## Scene VII

*Sunday, shortly after noon, through the glass of the patio doors in the living room can be seen a five-foot evergreen tree with snow packed all around its base. While the snow against the garage wall in the background is two feet high, the rest of the yard has been walked on or shovelled almost to the grass. Vithal and Jayant are standing near the patio door looking out, beer cans in hand. Sridhar is stretched on a couch.*

**JAYANT:** *(Looking at his right palm)* Jeesus, am I ever in for blisters! Right through the work gloves and all!

**VITHAL:** Growing soft, are we?

**JAYANT:** That tree weighs half a ton. And prickly as a porcupine too.

**SRIDHAR:** Man, what d'you expect if not blisters? You were shovelling like a demon was in you. Now, can you tell me all about this farewell present? I just drop by, for a minute, and next thing I know I am shovelling and snorting in the snow.

**JAYANT:** No farewells. I ain't going.

**SRIDHAR:** You crazy or something, man?

**VITHAL:** Or maybe sane for once. Our brother here has decided to go sandbagging instead, along St Mary's, or maybe St Norbert. Service before self. Tamasoma Jyotir Gamaya—from darkness lead me to light.

**JAYANT:** Cut it out, Vith. I am dropping out of the trip because Jim's girlfriend has joined the gang, and who wants to be saddled up with a girl, Jeesus, no way.

**VITHAL:** Pixie said something about you being her chauffeur.

**JAYANT:** That kid is a blabbermouth. I dunno what she's talking about. D'you think the ice would hold a coupla weeks? We sure packed that snow in. Should be like concrete for at least a while.

**VITHAL:** If the temp goes up to zero degrees midweek, as they expect, that would be the end of that. *(He waves at the tree.)* **JAYANT.** So what? *(Vehemently)* What does it matter how long it stands? The point is that it is there, beautiful and green for the length of its life. A day, a hundred thousand days, it is a question of what we do and are, during that time. This evergreen doesn't have one Christly use—it isn't even good as firewood—but it is there and it is green, it is beautiful.

**SRIDHAR:** And rootless.

**JAYANT:** Yeah, rootless. Let's face it, Jeesus, no one, but no one has roots anywhere because that's the way things are in 1979 A.D. But we can stand tall, man, and live each day for all it's godamned worth and ours. And now I'm going for a shower. Never thought one could sweat oneself to stink just shovelling snow.

*Doorbell rings. Jayant goes to the door and opens it. Veejala enters. Sridhar springs up as Jayant helps her out of her coat.*

**VEEJALA:** Have the pizzas been delivered? I'm sorry I'm late.

*Priti, Krish, Jyoti, and Anant have come in behind Veejala, carrying cartons of soft drinks and potato and taco chips.*

**VEEJALA:** *(Coming in)* Hullo Sridhar! Vithal, this is a wonderful surprise. We were so hoping you'd come home for dinner last night. I had borrowed Jyoti and Krish, seeing as I never get to have my own children with me. *(She embraces him.)* Sweetheart, have you been on a construction site? There's sawdust or something in your hair, and you've been perspiring. *(She runs her hand through his hair and embraces him again.)* Well, I got late picking up the kids from the skating rink, and so I ordered pizza delivered here. I knew Savi and Sharad would have gone to the temple today. They should be back any minute, and we are going to be one big happy family for one last time, until you come back, Jai.

**VITHAL:** News, news, Jayant is staying back.

**JAYANT:** Because Jim's girlfriend insists on coming and—

**SRIDHAR:** Who wants to be saddled with a girl?